Contents

Practice Multiple-choice Papers suitable for:

Key Skills Level 1 Communication;
Level 1 Adult Literacy (Basic Skills); and
ESOL Skills for Life Level 1 Reading

Roslyn Whitley Willis

Published by
Lexden Publishing Ltd
www.lexden-publishing.co.uk

A3 360 914 X

First Published in 2007 by Lexden Publishing Ltd.

ISBN: 978-1-904995-38-8

Lexden Publishing Ltd
23 Irvine Road
Colchester
Essex CO3 3TS

Email: info@lexden-publishing.co.uk
www.lexden-publishing.co.uk

Printed in Great Britain by Lightning Source

Introduction

This book provides a resource that can be used by both tutors who deliver, and students who are following a Key Skills and Adult Literacy (sometimes called Basic Skills) End Assessment at Level 1, or ESOL Skills for Life: Reading.

The difference between a Key Skills qualification and an Adult Literacy qualification

A Key Skills qualification is achieved by candidates who pass the externally-set and examined End Assessment paper and submit a successful Portfolio of Evidence.

An Adult Literacy qualification is awarded to candidates who pass the End Assessment paper, referred to as the National Adult Literacy test.

The End Assessment question paper for both qualifications is the same, as it is for ESOL Skills for Life Level 1 Reading.

What does an End Assessment for Key Skills and Adult Literacy examine?

The external assessment of both courses is in the form of a paper containing 40 multiple-choice questions. These papers aim to assess the candidates' ability to identify main points and ideas in written material; understand the purpose of documents and style of writing; interpret information in tables, graphs and charts; and recognize correct spelling, grammar and punctuation.

What the book contains and how to use it

This book contains 12 multiple-choice question papers, closely designed to resemble End Assessment question papers. Each paper contains 40 multiple-choice questions that test those aspects of the Standards described in the previous paragraph.

The distribution of skills tested by each of the 480 questions is tabled on *pages 180 to 182*. By including this analysis I have enabled users to easily a) select specific aspects to practise, and/or b) analyse areas of weakness from the responses to the questions. This is, of course, useful when determining which aspect needs to be strengthened before any multiple-choice paper is attempted.

It is expected that candidates, when ready to attempt a full paper, will work through each sample paper following the QCA guidelines of 1 hour and that conditions similar to the "live" End Assessment experience will prevail. Namely, the candidate is not allowed to use a dictionary; the candidate works alone, and; the candidate completes an Answer Sheet, an example of which is included on *page 183*. I am aware that some candidates will do an on-line test and thus they will have no involvement with the included style of Answer Sheet. However, for those who take a paper-based test, the style of the Answer Sheet included in this book will prepare them when they do the written test paper and I believe it is the easiest way for candidates to select their answers and for tutors to mark their responses.

The answers to each question, on each paper, are tabled on *pages 177 to 179*.

The "Pass" mark

For Key Skills and Adult Literacy, QCA guidelines suggest a pass mark of between 26 to 28 out of 40. This represents a pass percentage of 65 to 70. In practice, I always determine a "Pass" is represented by 29 to 30 out of 40, which is 72 to 75%. I do this because it allows candidates some "slippage" in the real test paper. Along with thorough coverage and practice of the Standards related to the test paper, it is an assessment criteria which I have never regretted adopting.

The importance of practising for the test paper

Always make sure that your candidates have the opportunity to practise many test papers. Practice does encourage an understanding of the techniques involved — reading carefully; analysing what is intended and for which audience; recognising spelling, grammar and punctuation errors; understanding and selecting the main points; and demonstrating a knowledge of correct document layout. Practice can engender confidence and competence. Competence does lead to success.

Practice Multiple-choice Paper
suitable for:

Key Skills Level 1 Communication;
Level 1 Adult Literacy (Basic Skills); and
ESOL Skills for Life Level 1 Reading

Paper One

YOU NEED
- This test paper.
- A pen.
- A pencil and eraser.
- An Answer Sheet.

You may NOT use a dictionary.
There are 40 questions on this paper. Try to answer ALL the questions.
When you have completed the questions you must check your answers,
then check them again.

YOU HAVE ONE HOUR TO FINISH THE PAPER

INSTRUCTIONS
- Make sure you write your name and today's date on the Answer Sheet. Use a pen to do this.
- Use a pencil to mark your answers so if you change your mind you can erase your choice and select another.
- Make sure that for each question you have only selected one answer. If you select more than one, the answer will not be marked.
- Read each question carefully before you select an answer.

Note for learners and tutors: This is a practice test that has been designed to closely resemble the questions and question styles of a "live" paper.

Questions 1 to 7 relate to **Canberra**

CANBERRA	
In June 1996 the shipping line P&O announced the withdrawal of *Canberra* cruise ship after 36 years' service as a cruise liner. The ship was to be withdrawn in September the following year.	Line 1
Canberra was introduced to the fleet in 1961 with an advertising campaign using the banner "The Ship that Shapes the Future".	Line 5
She was built for P&O by the Harland and Wolff shipyard in Newcastle upon Tyne and was designed by John West who was only 29 years of age.	
She had many features, unique at the time of her launch, including a cocktail bar called The Crow's Nest Bar. This had floor-to-ceiling windows overlooking the bows and reached via a circular marble staircase.	Line 10
Canberra saw service with the armed forces in 1982 when she travelled 25,245 nautical miles to and from the Falkland Islands and Southampton, from 8 April until 11 July, during the Falklands War. She carried 6,500 troops and 4,200 prisoners of war.	
During her time as a cruise liner, *Canberra* sailed 3,000,000 nautical miles and carried a million passengers.	Line 15

1   The word **withdrawal** appears in **Line 1**. What would be a suitable alternative word that could be used, without altering the meaning of the text?

   A   retreat
   B   removal
   C   arrival
   D   deposit

2   When did *Canberra* first enter service for P&O?

   A   1982
   B   1996
   C   1961
   D   1982

3   Where was *Canberra* built?

   A   Southampton
   B   Newcastle upon Tyne
   C   The Falkland Islands
   D   Australia

4 How many nautical miles did *Canberra* travel as a cruise liner?

   A   six thousand, five hundred
   B   three million
   C   thirty million
   D   four thousand, two hundred

5 What was the name of her cocktail bar?

   A   The John West
   B   The Staircase
   C   The Crow's Nest
   D   Harland and Wolff

6 The word **unique** is used on **Line 8**. What would be an alternative word that could be used without altering the meaning of the text?

   A   rare
   B   alternative
   C   assorted
   D   different

7 For how many months was she in service during the Falklands War?

   A   4
   B   3
   C   2
   D   5

Questions 8 to 15 relate to this business letter

FASHION MONTHLY

Haddington House
Nottingham
NT2 8SQ

01747 343227
FashionMonthly@haddington.co.uk

Miss Katie Bamber
18 Moray Place
Leith
EDINBURGH
ED14 2KP

Dear Miss Bamber

SUBSCRIPTION TO FASHION MONTHLY - SUBSCRIPTION NUMBER 18736J

Thank you for becoming a subscriber to **Fashion Weekly**. We are sure you will enjoy
this magazine and will be pleased you made the desision to subscribe. Your cheque for
£26.80 has been recieved and we are pleased to inform you that your subscription begins
with next months edition. You will receive 12 copies.

One of the benefits of subscribing is that you need never go to your Newsagent to
discover this popular magazine has been sold out. We deliver it to your door 3 days
before it arrives in the shops each month.

Throughout the year you will be able to take advantage of special offers which are only
available to subscribers. Please quote your subscription number when placing an order
for any of these offers.

We thank you again for taking this special interest in our magazine and wish you a happy
years reading.

Yours faithfully

Jenny Troutbeck

Jenny Troutbeck
Subscriptions Manager

8   What is missing from the letter before the name and address of the recipient?

   A   the company's website address
   B   the date
   C   the writer's name
   D   the company's fax number

9   What piece of information is incorrect in the **first paragraph** of the letter?

   A   the date the subscription begins
   B   the name of the magazine
   C   the subscription number
   D   the value of the cheque

10   There are two spelling errors in the first paragraph. Which words from the choices below would correct these errors?

   A   decision, check
   B   check, beggins
   C   decision, received
   D   received, addition

11   An apostrophe has been omitted from a word in the **first paragraph**. Which of the words shown below should be included to correct the error?

   A   You're
   B   begins'
   C   month's
   D   copies'

12   How many days before the magazine goes on sale in shops does a subscriber receive their magazine?

   A   3
   B   7
   C   8
   D   12

13 What is the cost of the subscription?

    A £12
    B £20
    C £26.08
    D £26.80

14 Which complimentary close should have been used?

    A Yours
    B Yours sincerely
    C Kind regards
    D Good wishes

15 Who wrote the letter?

    A Katie Bamber
    B Excelsior Cosmetics
    C Jennie Trowbeck
    D Jenny Troutbeck

Questions 16 to 20 relate to the text and graph **Flaming Heat Rub**

FLAMING HEAT : INTENSIVE RELIEF FOR MUSCULAR PAIN

FLAMING HEAT RUB

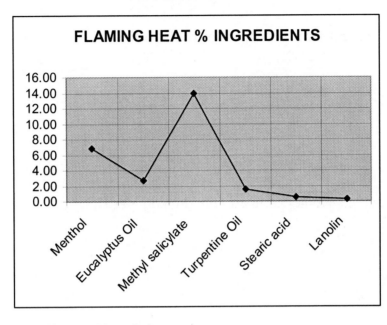

Do not use Flaming Heat Rub

- if you are allergic to any of the ingredients

- if you are allergic to any painkillers such as asprin

- on children younger than 5 years of age

If you are pregnant, consult your doctor before use.

How to use Flaming Heat Rub

Massage a thin layer gently into the affected area. It can be used before and after exercise. Apply 2-3 times daily.

Storage

Store below 24°C (reject if stored above this) and keep out of reach of children. Use before the "use by" date shown on the tube.

Manufactured by:
Hylton Chemicals, Perth, Scotland G86 3ST

16   Flaming Heat contains the largest amount of which ingredient?

    A   Methyl salicylate
    B   Eucalyptus Oil
    C   Menthol
    D   Menthol salicylate

17   How many ingredients are there in the rub that are over two percent?

    A   2
    B   3
    C   4
    D   5

18   What kind of container is used for Flaming Heat?

    A   jar
    B   tub
    C   tube
    D   pot

19   Which storage temperature would mean you would have to throw away Flaming Heat?

    A   23°
    B   22°
    C   20°
    D   24°

20   Under what circumstances should you consult a doctor before using the cream?

    A   if you are taking asprin
    B   if you are pregnant
    C   if you are allergic to any of the ingredients
    D   if you want to administer it to a child of 6

Questions 21 to 28 relate to this article

NAMING NEW ROADS	Line 1
It is important that developers of new estates should contact the local Council at an early stage in order that a street naming and numbering scheme can be agreed and approval issued to the developer by the Council.	
The Council will notify the Royal Mail who will issue post codes for the new development. No post codes are issued until the Council seeks permission from Royal Mail.	Line 5
***********	
A new street should be numbered with even numbers on one side and odd numbers on the other. Other points to note for new streets are:-	Line 10
When entering a street, odd numbers are on the left and even on the right.	
All streets will include the number 13, to be used in the proper sequence.	
Buildings on corner sites should be numbered according to the street in which the main entrance is located.	
All properties in a street should be numbered.	Line 15
The use of numbers followed by letters, for instance 12a, should only be used where one large building is demolished and replaced by several buildings. To include the new building in the existing numbering sequence would involve renumbering all the higher numbered buildings. In this case, 12a, 12b etc is permitted.	Line 20
Naming new roads	
New street names should not duplicate any similar name already in use in the area.	
Street names should not be difficult to pronounce, awkward to spell or open to misinterpretation.	Line 25

21   What does the Council encourage developers to do early in the process?

    A   make a decision about street names
    B   contact the Royal Mail
    C   contact the Council for permission related to street names and numbers
    D   decide how the buildings are to be numbered

22 What would be the most appropriate heading on **Line 8**?

    A   How to number new streets
    B   Building numbers
    C   Numbering streets
    D   Using odd and even numbers

23 If you are entering a street where would you expect to find property No 16?

    A   on the left hand side
    B   after number 15
    C   on the right hand side
    D   before number 15

24 The word **sequence** is used on **Line 12**. What alternative word could be used which does not alter the meaning of the text?

    A   layout
    B   chain
    C   system
    D   order

25 The word **duplicate** is used on **Line 22**. What alternative word could be used which does not alter the meaning of the text?

    A   copy
    B   replace
    C   identical
    D   matching

26 The word **misinterpretation** is used on **Line 25**. What alternative word could be used which does not alter the meaning of the text?

    A   problems
    B   misunderstanding
    C   confusing
    D   understanding

27 When is it possible to number buildings with a number followed by a letter?

    A   when the developer and the Council thinks it looks nice
    B   when one building replaces several
    C   when several buildings replace one building
    D   instead of using Number 13

28 What is the main purpose of the article?

    A   to give advice
    B   to answer questions
    C   to persuade
    D   to inform

Questions 29 to 31 relate to punctuation and spelling.

29 In which of the following sentences is the punctuation and spelling correct?

    A   In Febrary I'm going to Colledge to study buisness. I hope its intresting.
    B   In Febrary I'm going to College to study busness. I hope its' intresting.
    C   In Febuary I'm going to Colledge to studie business. I hope it's interesting.
    D   In February I'm going to College to study business. I hope it's interesting.

30 In which of the following sentences is the punctuation and spelling correct?

    A   Amelia and John joined the swimming clubs' 100m compatition. They're hoping to win a prize.
    B   Amelia and John joined the swimming clubs 100m competittion. Theyr'e hopeing to win a prize.
    C   Amelia and John joined the swimming club's 100m competition. They're hoping to win a prize.
    D   Amelia and John joyned the swimming clubs' 100m competition. The'yre hopeing to win a prize.

31 In which of the following sentences is the punctuation and spelling correct?

    A   The doctor's surgery has six doctors, but its still dificullt to get an appointment.
    B   The doctors' surgry has six doctors, but its' still difficullt to get an appointment.
    C   The doctors' surgery has six doctor's, but its still diffickult to get an apointtment.
    D   The doctors' surgery has six doctors, but it's still difficult to get an appointment.

Questions 32 to 34 refer to this advertisement

HOME LEARNING COURSES

Imagine gaining important knowledge and skills, which lead to a National qualification, in the comfort of your own home.

HLC offers over 60 supported home courses to help you gain better job prospects.

Some of the jobs for which we offer qualifications are shown in the list below.

Electrician
Legal secretary
Veterinary nurse
Health care assistant
Make-up artist
Interior decorator
Photographer
Pet groomer
Fitness instructor

Get the information you need by contacting:
08154 465 223
or visiting:
www.homelearningcourses.org.uk

---

32 If someone was interested in any of the courses, where would they study?

    A   at a Home Learning Centre
    B   at home
    C   via the internet
    D   at a local education centre

33 If the jobs were listed in alphabetical order, which would appear second on the list?

    A   Interior decorator
    B   Legal secretary
    C   Fitness instructor
    D   Make-up artist

34 How can information be obtained from the company?

    A   by telephone
    B   by the website and email
    C   by email
    D   by the website and telephone

Questions 35 to 40 relate to **Lundy**

LUNDY

Lundy lies off the coast of North Devon. It is where the Atlantic ocean meets the Bristol Channel. There is nothing between the island and America. It is 3½ miles long and ½ a mile wide, is 400 feet high and is peaceful and unspoilt.

DIVING OFF LUNDY

The Lundy Marine Nature reserve is superb for divers. Its clear waters are warmed by the Gulf Stream so colourful warm water species rarely found elsewhere in British waters can be seen off Lundy.

Many divers have had memorable encounters with the inquisitive grey seals which live around Lundy in the summer months, and some have even snorkelled with basking sharks.

The fierce currents and tides around the island mean that the diving is not for the novice diver.

THE BIRDS OF LUNDY

There are about 35 species which breed on the island. Most people associate Lundy with puffins - indeed the name Lundy means **Puffin Island**. It is still the only place in Devon where puffins breed.

35   How wide is the island of Lundy?

    A   3½ miles

    B   400 miles

    C   ½ mile

    D   4 miles

36   Why are the waters surrounding Lundy warm?

    A   they are sheltered

    B   they are warmed by the Gulf Stream

    C   the island does not get cold weather

    D   the island is near America

37   The word **encounters** is used in the second paragraph of **Diving Off Lundy**. What alternative word could be used without altering the meaning of the text?

    A   meetings

    B   stumbling

    C   diving

    D   thoughts

38   Apart from basking sharks what other creatures could a diver see in the summer months?

    A   dolphins
    B   whales
    C   grey seals
    D   turtles

39   The word **novice** is used in the final paragraph of **Diving Off Lundy**. What alternative word could be used without altering the meaning of the text?

    A   youngster
    B   experienced
    C   gentle
    D   beginner

40   Why are puffins so special to the island?

    A   because they are very pretty birds
    B   because it is the only place in Devon where they breed and Lundy means Puffin Island
    C   because Lundy has been associated with puffins for centuries
    D   because Lundy means Puffin Island

END OF PAPER ONE   END OF PAPER ONE   END OF PAPER ONE

Practice Multiple-choice Paper suitable for:

Key Skills Level 1 Communication; Level 1 Adult Literacy (Basic Skills); and ESOL Skills for Life Level 1 Reading

Paper Two

YOU NEED
- This test paper.
- A pen.
- A pencil and eraser.
- An Answer Sheet.

You may NOT use a dictionary.
There are 40 questions on this paper. Try to answer ALL the questions.
When you have completed the questions you must check your answers, then check them again.

YOU HAVE ONE HOUR TO FINISH THE PAPER

INSTRUCTIONS
- Make sure you write your name and today's date on the Answer Sheet. Use a pen to do this.
- Use a pencil to mark your answers so if you change your mind you can erase your choice and select another.
- Make sure that for each question you have only selected one answer. If you select more than one, the answer will not be marked.
- Read each question carefully before you select an answer.

Note for learners and tutors: This is a practice test that has been designed to closely resemble the questions and question styles of a "live" paper.

Questions 1 to 10 relate to the text **Countryside Walks**

COUNTRYSIDE WALKS SERIES — MAP NUMBER 23 of 30

ASHTON LE SKERNES

This walk covers 14 miles.

The area was owned, in the 1300s, by Herbert Newton - Lord Ashton - but in the 19th Century the area had become the property of Lord Skernes.

Countryside Code

- Please keep to the footpaths and bridleways.
- Please ensure dogs are under close control at all times.
- Take your litter home with you.
- Remember to close all gates.

Following the walk

The map, overleaf, shows the network of footpaths, bridleways and roads around Ashton le Skernes (1¼ miles west of Northton le Skernes). From this map you can select your own route.

Please note the following before setting out:

- footpaths are marked in yellow
- bridleways are marked in blue
- motorbikes and cars are **not** permitted on any footpaths or bridleways
- cyclists and horse riders may use any of the lanes and bridleways marked on the map
- Lime Lane, Oak Lane and Ash Wynd can be quite busy with vehicles travelling at speed so please take especial care
- at present the footpath running north from Ashton le Skernes crosses the East Coast Main Line. Take great care. In the future the path may be diverted under a tunnel.

LE SKERNES DISTRICT COUNCIL
Council Offices
Northton le Skernes

1   In which century did the transfer of the ownership of the land take place?

      A   12th
      B   19th
      C   20th
      D   13th

2   How many things does the walker need to remember in the Countryside Code?

      A   1
      B   2
      C   3
      D   4

3   How long is the Ashton le Skernes walk?

      A $1\frac{1}{4}$ miles
      B   14 miles
      C   23 miles
      D   11 miles

4   Who first owned the land?

      A   Herbert Ashton
      B   Lord Skernes
      C   Le Skernes District Council
      D   Lord Ashton

5   On the map how would a walker recognise bridleways?

      A   they are marked in yellow
      B   they are marked with a dotted line
      C   they are marked in blue
      D   they are marked with the letter B

6   What is not permitted on footpaths and bridleways?

      A   running
      B   children
      C   cyclists and horse riders
      D   motorbikes and cars

7 When the text says the "footpath from Ashton le Skernes crosses the **East Coast Main Line**", what does this mean?

    A the path runs along the east coast
    B there are main roads going east across the path
    C there is a main railway line crossing the path
    D the path crosses the main east coast railway line

8 Where is the walker advised to take care of speeding vehicles?

    A on bridleways
    B in Lime Lane, Oak Lane and Ash Wynd
    C on the footpath north of Ashton le Skernes
    D in Northton le Skernes

9 How many walks are in the series published by Le Skernes District Council?

    A hundreds
    B 23
    C 30
    D 14

10 What is the purpose of the text?

    A to advise
    B to advertise
    C to warn
    D to inform

Questions 11 to 17 are about the text **Win a Car**

ONE LUCKY READER HAS THE CHANCE TO WIN A SUPER SPORTY
"ALICANTE MODEL 1"

Do'nt be mislead by its compact size, the **Alicante Model 1** is spacious, has alloy wheels, a 1.3 litre engine, air conditioning and leather-trim seats*.

Its worth £8,700 and comes **complete with a year's free insurance and road tax**.

To win, just email us, before 30th September, at alicante1@carshop.com and tell us, in fewer than 35 words, why you would like to win this car.**
The winner will be notified by email on 5th October.

* The car is offered in Post Office red with grey cloth seats which have black leather trim.

** Entrants must be over 18 years of age and hold a full UK driving licence.

---

11   What model car is being offered as the prize?

    A   Super Sporty
    B   Alicante Super Sporty
    C   Super Sporty Alicante
    D   Alicante Model 1

12 There is a punctuation error in the first paragraph. Which word would be needed to correct the error?

- **A** Donn't
- **B** Don't
- **C** its'
- **D** it's

13 The word **spacious** is used in the first paragraph. Which alternative word could be used, without changing the meaning of the text?

- **A** comfortable
- **B** luxurious
- **C** roomy
- **D** economical

14 Which best describes the seats in the car?

- **A** red cloth with black leather trim
- **B** grey cloth with black leather trim
- **C** grey leather with black leather trim
- **D** grey with red leather trim

15 There is a punctuation error in the second paragraph. Which word would be needed to correct the error?

- **A** Its'
- **B** It's
- **C** years'
- **D** years

16 How does a person enter the competition?

- **A** email by 5th October in 35 words
- **B** email before 5th October in no more than 35 words
- **C** email before 30th September, using 35 words
- **D** email before 30th September using fewer than 35 words

17 What conditions apply to entrants?

- **A** they must be over 18 and have a full UK driving licence
- **B** they must be over 21
- **C** they must be over 21 and have a full UK driving licence
- **D** they must be over 18 and have a UK driving licence

Questions 18 to 22 relate to **Today's Racing**

TODAY'S RACING

Racecourse	Race Times	Favourite Horse
Leicester	2.00 3.00 4.30	Folio Ice Cap Moonshadow
Sedgefield	1.30 2.15 3.30	The European The Bollin Resplendent
Carlisle	1.30 3.00 5.00	Aida Blu Jenny Wren Thornaby Green
York	1.15 2.45 3.30	City Walls Lendal Bridge Royal Challenge
Thirsk	1.30 2.30 4.30	Ginger Biscuit Inch Forward A Cadeira
Chester	4.30 5.45 7.00	Walton Thames Aida Diva Cruise Liner
Doncaster	11.30 1.30 2.45	Sethton Black Bandit Trampus

18   If the Racecourses were arranged in alphabetical order, which would come third?

   A   Doncaster
   B   Carlisle
   C   Sedgefield
   D   Chester

19   At which racecourse is the **latest** race run?

   A   Doncaster
   B   Carlisle
   C   Chester
   D   Leicester

20 How many racecourses have a 3pm race?

    A   1
    B   2
    C   3
    D   4

21 How many racecourses have a 4.30 race?

    A   1
    B   2
    C   3
    D   4

22 Which racecourses have horses whose names begin with the letter **A**?

    A   Chester, York and Thirsk
    B   Chester, Leicester and York
    C   Carlisle, Thirsk and Chester
    D   Chester, Sedgefield and York

Questions 23 to 30 relate to this text

Brookshire County Council

DISPLAY OF GOODS AND A-BOARDS ON THE HIGHWAY

Brookshire County Council has a duty to protect the rights of the public to use any highway for which they are responsible. It is an offence to block the highway so as to cause a nuisance.

Display of goods and the placing of A-boards outside retail premises can block a footpath or highway.

Of particular concern to Brookshire County Council is where goods or an A-board:

- prevent the free passage of pedestrians, whether able-bodied or not;
- cause a nuisance;
- form a danger (including a danger caused by blocking the view) to users of the highway.

COUNTY COUNCIL POLICY

Goods or A-boards placed on any footway or within the highway verge will be checked on a monthly basis to ensure that nuisance or danger is not being caused to highway users.

BCC is especially aware of the needs of visually impaired pedestrians, persons confined to wheelchairs and electrically-powered scooters, and adults with children in pushchairs.

Where offenders brake of the Highways Act 1980, they will be notified verbally of possible offences being committed and advised what steps are required in order to put right the problem.

If you require further information, write to us at our address:
The Highways Department, Brookshire County Council, County Hall, Brookshire, Suffolk

If you require this information in other languages, telephone:
01834 381 661

23 For whom is the information mainly intended?

   A   retailers/shop keepers
   B   shoppers
   C   local Councils
   D   the Police

24 The word **offence** is used in the first paragraph. Which alternative word could be used without altering the meaning of the text?

A problem
B order
C crime
D assist

25 How often does the Council check to see if the highway is obstructed?

A weekly
B yearly
C monthly
D daily

26 The initials BCC are used in a number of places in the text. What do they stand for?

A Berkshire County Council
B Bookham County Council
C Brookshire Council Concerns
D Brookshire County Council

27 There is a spelling error in the final paragraph of the side heading **County Council Policy**. Which word would need to be inserted in order to correct this error?

A We're
B Were
C break
D comitted

28 If a reader wanted more information what would they do?

A telephone the Council Highways Department
B make an appointment to visit the Council
C write to the Council
D email the Council

29 How could the content of the leaflet be described?

A threatening
B persuasive
C informative
D confusing

30 Why would a reader of the information telephone the Council?

    A   to get further information
    B   to request the leaflet in a language other than English
    C   to complain about a retailer blocking the highway
    D   to take legal action

Questions 31 and 32 relate to the table and the charts/graphs below

MONTH	NUMBER OF RETAILERS SERVED WITH NOTICES
March	6
April	11
May	3
June	7
July	12
August	8

A

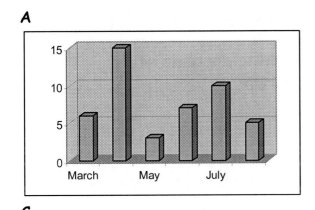

B

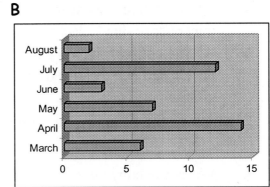

C

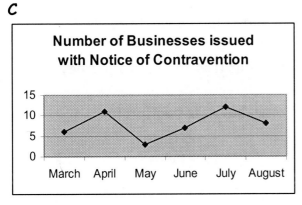

D

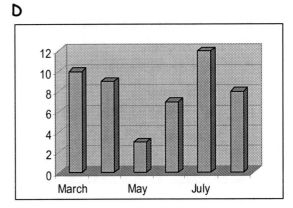

31 Which of the graphs/charts accurately represents the information shown in the table?

    A   A
    B   B
    C   C
    D   D

32 What does each graph/chart need in order to help the reader understand the information?

    A   a title
    B   axes labels
    C   a legend
    D   a title and axes labels

Questions 33 and 34 relate to spelling

33 In which of the following sentences are all the words spelt correctly?

    A   At the concert we were seated seperately because we perchased our tickets at the last minutte.
    B   At the concert we where seated separately because we perchased our tickets at the last minuet.
    C   At the concert we were seated separately because we purchassed our tickets at the last minute.
    D   At the concert we were seated separately because we purchased our tickets at the last minute.

34 In which of the following sentences are all the words spelt correctly?

    A   We ocasionally visit Pam and Peter, but it is to far to journey each week.
    B   We ocassionly visit Pam and Peter, but it is two far to journie each weak.
    C   We occasionally visit Pam and Peter, but it is too far to journey each week.
    D   We occasionalley visit Pam and Peter, but it is two far to journey each weak.

Questions 35 to 40 relate to the text **Ironing**

IRONING

Household technology has finally produced the answer to every womans prayers – a washing machine which washes clothes and irons them.

The machine works by blasting the garment with steam and twenty minutes after washing, it emerges minus creases.

The machine is manufactured by a Japanese company and has been on the market in Japan since late 2005.

A disadvantage is that a full washing load takes two and a half hours to wash and iron the items. The manufacturers say the use of steam cuts down power and water consumption and will appeal to those who are environmentally-conscious. This is because the machine uses 35 per cent less water, and 21 per cent less electricity than conventional washing machines.

Available in Britain from June 2006 in black, cherry, aqua blue, rose and white, it costs £900, more than double the price of a conventional washing machine.

35 There is a punctuation error in the first paragraph. Which word would need to be included in order to correct the error?

A woman's

B women's

C prayers'

D iron's

36 What is seen as a disadvantage to the new machine?

    A   it does not remove all the creases
    B   a full load cycle takes two and a half hours
    C   it uses more water
    D   it uses more water and electricity

37 In how many colours is the new machine available?

    A   2
    B   3
    C   4
    D   5

38 The phrase "appeal to" appears in the fourth paragraph. What alternative word could be used without altering the meaning of the text?

    A   interest
    B   ask
    C   please
    D   influence

39 The word "conventional" is used in the last paragraph. What alternative word could be used without altering the meaning of the text?

    A   current
    B   usual
    C   general
    D   abnormal

40 When was the machine available in Japan?

    A   early in 2005
    B   in June 2006
    C   late 2005
    D   since late 2006

END OF PAPER TWO   END OF PAPER TWO   END OF PAPER TWO

Practice Multiple-choice Paper
suitable for:

Key Skills Level 1 Communication;
Level 1 Adult Literacy (Basic Skills); and
ESOL Skills for Life Level 1 Reading

Paper Three

YOU NEED
- This test paper.
- A pen.
- A pencil and eraser.
- An Answer Sheet.

You may NOT use a dictionary.
There are 40 questions on this paper. Try to answer ALL the questions.
When you have completed the questions you must check your answers,
then check them again.

YOU HAVE ONE HOUR TO FINISH THE PAPER

INSTRUCTIONS
- Make sure you write your name and today's date on the Answer Sheet. Use a pen to do this.
- Use a pencil to mark your answers so if you change your mind you can erase your choice and select another.
- Make sure that for each question you have only selected one answer. If you select more than one, the answer will not be marked.
- Read each question carefully before you select an answer.

Note for learners and tutors: This is a practice test that has been designed to closely resemble the questions and question styles of a "live" paper.

Questions 1 to 10 relate to this text

FARMERS MARKETS

Lincolnshire has many market towns that boast both traditional regular markets and specialised farmers markets.

Whisby	Coleby
Third Friday of each month	Fourth Wednesday of each month
Location: Post House Wynd	Location: High Street
Bassingham	**Cherry Willingham**
Second Saturday of each month	Every Monday
Location: Westgate	Location: High Street
Ryland	**Holton cum Beckering**
Second Saturday of each month	Every Thursday
Location: Barton Square	Location: Chapel Meadows Park
Glentworth	**Toft next Newton**
Last Sunday of each month	First Sunday of each month
Location: High Street	Location: Parkwood Square

The markets supply communitys with food produced locally, home bargains, clothing and crafts.

1   There is a punctuation error in the title. Which word would be needed to correct this error?

    A   farmer's
    B   markets'
    C   market's
    D   farmers'

2   How many towns/villages hold markets?

    A   5
    B   6
    C   7
    D   8

3   In which county are these towns/villages?

    A   North Yorkshire
    B   Cumbria
    C   Lincolnshire
    D   Essex

4   How many towns/villages hold the markets in the High Street location?

    A   1
    B   2
    C   3
    D   4

5   There is a spelling error in the final two lines. Which word would be needed in order to correct this error?

    A   community's
    B   bargains'
    C   bargens
    D   communities

6   Which statement is true?

    A   Markets are held in two places on a Thursday
    B   Markets are held in two places on a Saturday, both on the second Saturday of every month.
    C   Markets are held in two places on the second Sunday of every month.
    D   Three markets are held on a Saturday, two on the second Saturday of every month and one on the first Saturday of every month

7   The tone of the text can be described as

    A   interesting
    B   confusing
    C   encouraging
    D   informative

8 If the town/village names were arranged alphabetically in one column, which town/village would be placed second?

    A   Coleby
    B   Cherry Willingham
    C   Glentworth
    D   Ryland

9 Which of the following statements is true?

    A   Glentworth holds its market on the first Sunday of each month in the High Street.
    B   Toft next Newton holds a market in Parkwood Square on the first Sunday of every month
    C   Cherry Willingham and Glentworth hold their markets in the High Street on the last Sunday of every month
    D   Bassingham and Ryland hold markets on the second of every month in Westgate and Barton Square.

10 How many types of items are sold in the markets?

    A   4
    B   3
    C   2
    D   1

Questions 11 to 19 relate to the Pets Safe At Home Booking Chart

PETS SAFE AT HOME

PET BOOKINGS - *SEPTEMBER*

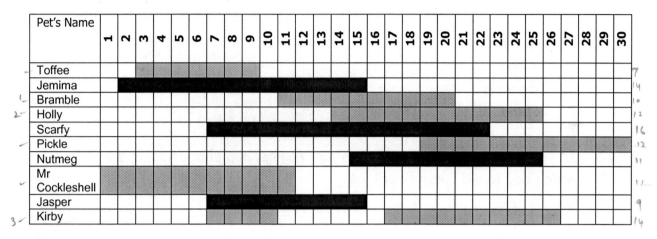

KEY

Cat
Dog

Owner	Pet	Owner	Pet
Mr and Mrs H Machin	Bramble	Miss Cartwright	Mr Cockleshell
Mr and Mrs G Fox	Holly	Dr and Mrs P Risby	Nutmet
Mr C Rosseton	Jasper	The Rev P Yarrow	Pickle
Miss P Pennitone	Jemima	Miss J Jewitt	Scarfy
Mrs I Winterton	Kirby	Mr K Underwood	Toffee

11   To which month does the Pet Bookings Sheet refer?

    A   June

    B   September

    C   March

    D   July

12   How many cats are booked into Pets Safe at Home?

    A   10

    B   7

    C   6

    D   4

13 Which animal(s) will have two visits in the month?

    A   Kirby the dog

    B   Kirby the cat and Jemima the dog

    C   Holly the cat and Nutmeg the dog

    D   Kirby the cat

14 Which pet will spend the most number of days at Pets Safe at Home?

    A   Jemima

    B   Kirby

    C   Scarffy

    D   Holly

15 If you were to arrange only the dogs' names, in alphabetical order, which dog would come **first**?

    A   Toffee

    B   Pickle

    C   Jasper

    D   Scarffy

16 If the owners' names were arranged in alphabetical order, which owner would come **last**?

    A   Dr Risby

    B   The Reverend Yarrow

    C   Mrs Winterton

    D   Mr Underwood

17 If the cats' names were arranged in alphabetical order, which would come **third** in the list?

    A   Holly

    B   Pickle

    C   Kirby

    D   Toffee

18 How many days is there **not** an animal in Pets Safe at Home?

    A   3

    B   0

    C   1

    D   2

19 Which of the following statements is true?

    A   Mr Cockleshell is a cat, is owned by Mrs Winterton and will be staying for 10 days.

    B   Toffee is a cat, is owned by The Reverend Yarrow and will be staying for 7 days.

    C   Jemima is a dog, is owned by Mrs Pennitone and will be staying for 14 days.

    D   Kirby is a cat, is owned by Mrs Winterton and will be staying, in total, for 14 days.

Questions 20 to 24 relate to this document

For		From	
Name	*Colin Ord*	Name	*Pheobe Green*
Dept	*Accounts*	Company	*Premier Motors*
		Contact Details	*5653 349200*
Taken by	*Heather Heath*		
Time	*11:05*		
Day/Date	*Wednesday, 22 November 2007*		

Re: Your car taken in for a service this morning

Pheobe Green of Premier Motors says the mechanical team has found a problem with the breaks and parts will have to be ordered if you agree to the repair. This means you cannot have your vehical back today.

She knows you need a car and if yours is to be repaired, it will not be ready until 28 November but Premier Motors can let you have a courtesy car.

Please telephone her with your decision

20 What kind of document is this?

    A   a memorandum

    B   a letter

    C   a report

    D   a telephone message

21 Who will receive the document?

    A   Pheobe Green

    B   Colin Ord

    C   Heather Heath

    D   the Accounts Department

22 There are two spelling errors in the first paragraph. Which words should be included to correct these errors?

    A   mechanicle, vehicel

    B   brakes, reppair

    C   reppair, vehicle

    D   brakes, vehicle

23 When will the owner's car be ready if the work is carried out?

    A   today

    B   22 November

    C   28 November

    D   27 November

24 What is Premier Motors offering to do?

    A   repair the car free of charge

    B   repair the car today

    C   repair the car and provide a courtesy car

    D   provide a courtesy car

Questions 25 to 27 relate to punctuation, grammar and spelling

25 In which of the following sentences is the spelling correct?

    A   I disgust the matter with Alan and he agrede with me that we must cansel the concert.

    B   ·I disgust the mater with Alan and he agreed with me that we must cancle the consert.

    C   I discussed the matter with Alan and he agreed with me that we must cansel the concert.

    D   I discussed the matter with Alan and he agreed with me that we must cancel the concert.

26 In which of the following sentences is the punctuation correct?

    A   The Midshire Councils' elected member's will vote on Thursday.

    B   The Midshire Councils elected members' will vote on Thursday.

    C   The Midshire Council's elected members will vote on Thursday.

    D   The Midshire Council's elected member's will vote on Thursday.

27 In which of the following sentences is the punctuation, grammar and spelling correct?

    A   Happily Jasmine's examinatian results are exellent and her mothers' delighted.

    B   Hapilly Jasmines examinasion results is excellent and her mother's delighted.

    C   Happily Jasmines' examination result's are excellent and her mother's delighted.

    D   Happily Jasmine's examination results are excellent and her mother's delighted.

Questions 28 to 34 relate to this text about being a blood donor

---

YOUR GUIDE TO BEING A BLOOD DONOR

DID YOU KNOW?

- Each blood donation you make can save up to three people's lives.
- Your blood is grouped, labelled, processed, tested and ready to use within 48 hours of your donation.
- The National Blood Service collects about 2 million donations every year to treat hospital patients.
- You can give blood every 16 weeks, which is three times a year.
- There are hundreds of donation sessions every week, running every day of the year except Christmas Day and New Year's Day.
- Existing donors can give blood until they are 70 years old.

THANK YOU FOR READING THIS AND FOR DECIDING TO BE A NATIONAL BLOOD DONOR

---

28 How can the document **best** be described?

    A   interesting

    B   amusing

    C   persuasive

    D   factual

29   How many things happen to donated blood before it is ready for use within 48 hours of donation?

  A   3
  B   4
  C   5
  D   6

30   How many donations are collected each year to treat hospital patients?

  A   2 million
  B   about 2 million
  C   hundreds
  D   12 million

31   How many days each year is there no donor service operating?

  A   1
  B   2
  C   3
  D   4

32   What is the maximum age for being a blood donor?

  A   35
  B   65
  C   70
  D   60

33   How many times each year can a donor give blood?

  A   16
  B   2
  C   3
  D   11

34   How many people's lives can one blood donation save?

  A   70
  B   3
  C   2 million
  D   2

Questions 35 to 39 relate to **Super Sward Lawn Master**

SUPER SWARD \
LAWN MASTER |
500G

CORDLESS
RECHARGEABLE
LAWN MOWER
ONLY £119
(plus p&p)

No messy, polluting petrol or oil is needed in this revolutionary
cordless lawn mower from Super Sward.
No fumes and no dangerous trailing wires.

*Like all our mowers, the 500G runs off a 12v rechargeable battery that
takes up to only 1 hour to recharge.*
It will cut 2500^2 m of lawn before needing to be recharged.

<u>Unique to this new design</u>
The 500G weighs 15kg and has a 25 litre grass bin

Buy this Super Sward 500G today
at the offer price of
£119 + p&p*
We guarantee delivery within 4 working days.
This mower normally retails for £189.99

To order:
telephone 07883 465 466
or visit
superswardlawncompany.co.uk/500g
and order online

* p&p £5.00

35   How much would a purchaser have to pay, including postage and
packing, to get a Lawn Master 500G?

    A   £119.00
    B   £189.00
    C   £124.00
    D   £124.00

36   What area of lawn will the Lawn Master 500G cut before it needs recharging?

   A   500 metres
   B   2500 metres
   C   25,000 square metres
   D   2,500 square metres

37   Other than the weight of the mower, what feature is included in part of the **new design**?

   A   a 12v rechargeable battery
   B   no fumes
   C   a 25 litre grass bin
   D   it takes only 1 hour to recharge

38   How many days will it take to receive the mower once ordered?

   A   within 4 working days
   B   7 – 10 days
   C   not more than 5
   D   3 days

39   In how many ways can the mower be ordered?

   A   1
   B   2
   C   3
   D   5

Question 40 refers to this catalogue and the Order Forms A, B, C and D

PETS SAFE AT HOME CHRISTMAS CATALOGUE SALE OFFERS

ITEM NO	DESCRIPTION	PRICE PER UNIT
13678	Santa Card Holder	£10.00
33990	Advent Box	£10.00
39009	Berry Wreath	£11.00
28098	Winter Berries Design Wrap and Tags	£5.00
49889	Collie Dog Calendar	£3.00
50090	Labrador Dog Calendar	£5.00
67835	Fruit Bon Bons	£4.00
75320	Cat Door Mat	£10.00
87245	Cat Design Sewing Basket	£25.00
77709	Fleece Scarf and Hat with Dog Motif	£17.00
45201	Mug and Coaster Set	£3.00
38888	Luxury Wool Wrap	£40.00

40 Mrs Hartley of Bexhill on Sea decides to buy some of the items advertised in the Pets Safe at Home catalogue. She wants:

- 2 collie dog calendars
- An advent box
- A cat door mat.

Which of the Order Forms has she competed correctly?

A   A
B   B
C   C
D   D

Order Form A

Qty	Item No					Description	Price	Item Total
1	3	3	9	9	0	Advent Box	£10.00	£10.00
2	4	9	9	8	9	Collie Dog Calendar	£3.00	£3.00
1	7	5	3	2	0	Cat Door Mat	£10.00	£10.00
							TOTAL	£23.00
Name	Mrs M Hartley							
Address	Seven Trees Cottage, Pear Tree Lane, Bexhill on Sea, Sussex BX4 7AP							
Return to: **Pets Safe at Home, Whiskers House, Pawsley, West Yorkshire WY23 9SC**								

Order Form B

Qty	Item No					Description	Price	Item Total
2	4	9	8	8	0	Collie Dog Calendar	£3.00	£6.00
1	3	3	9	9	0	Advent Calendar	£10.00	£10.00
1	7	5	3	2	0	Cat Door Mat	£10.00	£12.00
							TOTAL	£28.00
Name	Mrs M Hartley							
Address	Seven Trees Cottage, Pear Tree Lane, Bexhill on Sea, Sussex BX4 7AP							
Return to: **Pets Safe at Home, Whiskers House, Pawsley, West Yorkshire WY23 9SC**								

Order Form C

Qty	Item No					Description	Price	Item Total
1	3	3	9	9	0	Advent Box	£10.00	£10.00
1	4	9	8	8	9	Collie Dog Calendar	£3.00	£3.00
1	8	7	2	4	5	Cat Door Mat	£10.00	£10.00
							TOTAL	£23.00
Name	Mrs M Hartley							
Address	Seven Trees Cottage, Pear Tree Lane, Bexhill on Sea, Sussex BX4 7AP							
Return to: **Pets Safe at Home, Whiskers House, Pawsley, West Yorkshire WY23 9SC**								

Order Form D

Qty	Item No					Description	Price	Item Total
1	7	5	3	2	0	Cat Door Mat	£10.00	£10.00
2	4	9	8	8	9	Collie Dog Calendar	£3.00	£6.00
1	3	3	9	9	0	Advent Box	£10.00	£10.00
							TOTAL	£26.00
Name	Mrs M Hartley							
Address	Seven Trees Cottage, Pear Tree Lane, Bexhill on Sea, Sussex BX4 7AP							
Return to: **Pets Safe at Home, Whiskers House, Pawsley, West Yorkshire WY23 9SC**								

END OF PAPER THREE   END OF PAPER THREE

END OF PAPER THREE

Practice Multiple-choice Paper
suitable for:

Key Skills Level 1 Communication;
Level 1 Adult Literacy (Basic Skills); and
ESOL Skills for Life Level 1 Reading

Paper Four

YOU NEED
- This test paper.
- A pen.
- A pencil and eraser.
- An Answer Sheet.

You may NOT use a dictionary.
There are 40 questions on this paper. Try to answer ALL the questions.
When you have completed the questions you must check your answers,
then check them again.

YOU HAVE ONE HOUR TO FINISH THE PAPER

INSTRUCTIONS
- Make sure you write your name and today's date on the Answer Sheet. Use a pen to do this.
- Use a pencil to mark your answers so if you change your mind you can erase your choice and select another.
- Make sure that for each question you have only selected one answer. If you select more than one, the answer will not be marked.
- Read each question carefully before you select an answer.

Note for learners and tutors: This is a practice test that has been designed to closely resemble the questions and question styles of a "live" paper.

Questions 1 to 10 relate to the London Eye and the Yorkshire Eye

THE LONDON EYE	Line 1
The London Eye can carry 800 passengers per resolution and that's the same as 11 red London double-decker buses. Passengers on each flight can see up to 40 kilometers in all directions, when the weather permits.	
The London Eye opened in March 2000 and since that time has become a landmark in the city.	Line 5
It is visited by over 3.5 million people a year.	
THE YORKSHIRE EYE	
The National Railway Museum in the city of York also has a giant weel tourist attraction. The city's London-style eye opened on 20 January 2006 and is 60 metres high. Passengers on this attraction can see for 20 miles. It is the second tallest structure in York and is just 10 metres lower than the Lantern Tower in York Minster.	Line 10
It has 43 capsules, which can each hold eight passengers. This is a total of 344.	
THE LONDON EYE OPENING TIMES*	Line 15
Winter (October to May) 10:00 – 16:00 daily **Summer (June to September)** 10:00 – 21:00 daily	
* except 25 December	

1   How can the text best be described?

    A   opinion

    B   interesting

    C   factual

    D   argumentative

2   The word **permits** is used in **Line 4**. What alternative word could be used without altering the meaning of the text?

    A   subjects

    B   allows

    C   clears

    D   organises

3   How many passengers can the bigger of the two attractions hold?

    A   800

    B   1000

    C   344

    D   60

4 There is a spelling error in **Line 9**. Which word would need to be included in order to correct this error?

    A   National

    B   Museam

    C   gyant

    D   wheel

5 How far can passengers hope to see from the London Eye?

    A   40 miles

    B   40 kilometers

    C   20 kilometers

    D   20 miles

6 How many years after the London Eye did the Yorkshire Eye open?

    A   4

    B   5

    C   6

    D   2

7 What is the highest structure in York?

    A   York Minster

    B   the Yorkshire Wheel

    C   the Lantern Tower of York Minster

    D   the National Railway Museum

8 The London Eye opens in Winter and Summer. When does Summer begin for the attraction?

    A   1st May

    B   1st June

    C   31st May

    D   30th June

9 At what time does the London Eye close in Winter?

    A   6 pm

    B   3 pm

    C   4 pm

    D   5 pm

10 Which of the following statements is true?

A The London Eye opens every day of the year except Christmas Day.

B The Yorkshire Eye is 60 metres high and the tallest structure in the city.

C Passengers on the London Eye can usually see for 20 miles in all directions.

D The London Eye opened in April 2000 and has become a landmark in the city.

Questions 11 to 15 relate to the document **Junk Food Advertisements**

JUNK FOOD ADVERTISEMENTS **Possible new legislation for TV advertising**	Line 1
The Government is to consider extending advertising restrictions, which relate to how products are advertised, to cover junk and fast food.	
The Food Standards agency (FSA) wants a ban on the advertising of junk food on television before 9 pm.	Line 5
The FSA is in dispute with Ofcom, the broadcast regulator, which plans only to ban junk food advertisments during programmes specifically aimed at children.	
The focus on junk food advertising has grown recently out of the Government's concern over the increeseing number of children in the UK who are classed as obese. The latest figures show that the UK has the highest rates in Europe, with nearly a third of children under 16 regarded as overweight, and one in six as obese.	Line 10

11 The word **restrictions** appears in **Line 3** of the text. Which alternative word could be used without changing the meaning of the text?

A limits
B boundaries
C demands
D rules

12 What do the initials **FSA** stand for?

A Food Standard Authority
B Food Standards Action
C Food Standards Agency
D Fastfood Standards Agents

13 There is a spelling error in the **third paragraph**. Which word would be needed to correct this error?

A   disspute

B   regulater

C   witch

D   advertisements

14 There is a spelling error in the **final paragraph**. Which word would be needed to correct this error?

A   fokus

B   recentley

C   increasing

D   nearley

15 What does the FSA want to happen?

A   a ban on advertising junk food on television

B   an increase in advertising junk food on television

C   the number of children classed as obese to be reduced

D   a ban on advertising junk food on television before 9 pm

Questions 16 to 20 relate to this chart

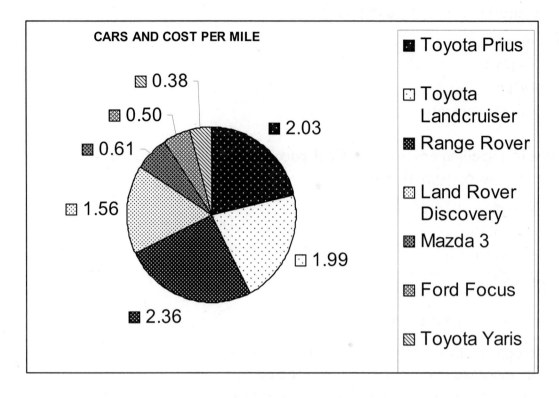

CARS AND COST PER MILE

0.38
0.50
0.61
2.03
1.56
1.99
2.36

- Toyota Prius
- Toyota Landcruiser
- Range Rover
- Land Rover Discovery
- Mazda 3
- Ford Focus
- Toyota Yaris

16 Which vehicle costs the **least** per mile to run?

A Range Rover
B Ford Focus
C Toyota Yaris
D Mazda 3

17 Which two vehicles cost the **most** per mile to run?

A Toyota Land Cruiser and Range Rover
B Toyota Prius and Land Rover Discovery
C Range Rover and Toyota Land Cruiser
D Toyota Prius and Range Rover

18 How many vehicles cost **less than £1 a mile** to run?

A 4
B 3
C 2
D 5

19   Which car manufacturer has the most cars listed on the chart?

   A   Toyota
   B   Mazda
   C   Ford
   D   Range Rover

A

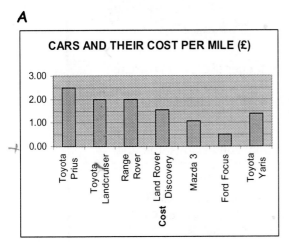

B

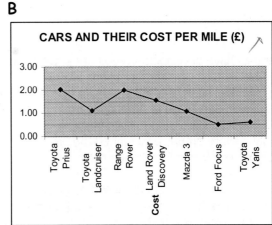

C

D

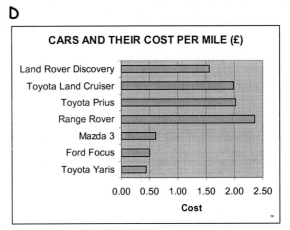

20   Which of the above charts/graphs accurately represents the information shown in the Pie Chart?

   A   A
   B   B
   C   C
   D   D

Questions 21 to 29 relate to this text

A NEW BREED OF CAT THAT

WON'T MAKE YOU SNEEZE

Help for the one in ten who have an allergy to cats

Scientists have developed a breed of cat which will not trigger allergies in humans.

The cats cost nearly £8,000 and have been created by a genetic engineering company in San Diego in America.

Animal welfare groups condemned the breeding programme and warned that the "designer pet" could face health risks.

Apparently allergy to cats is caused by a protein in the cat's skin which can trigger an allergic reaction if breathed in by sufferers of asthma. The allergy can cause chest complaints and rashes. Scientists in San Diego studied cats' genes in order to identify those with proteins which did **not** cause a reaction in humans. The scientists bred cats over several generations and produced more than 20 allergy-free offspring.

There is a two-year waiting list for intrested owners. The cats weigh up to 5lb and are mature at three years of age.

The RSPCA said that "selective breeding" and "genetic modification" could produce health problems which would not necessarily become clear in the short term.

21   How many people does the article suggest have an allergy to cats?

A   20
B   two out of ten
C   one in ten
D   nine out of ten

22   How many of these new type of cats have been bred?

A   5
B   10
C   8000
D   more than 20

23   What is the cost of these cats?

    A   £2,000
    B   £5,000
    C   approximately £8,000
    D   nearly £8,000

24   The word "trigger" is used in the fourth paragraph. Which alternative word could be used without altering the meaning of the text?

    A   halt
    B   start
    C   alter
    D   alert

25   What causes the allergy to cats?

    A   their fur
    B   their whiskers
    C   their skin
    D   a protein in the cat's skin

26   How much is it expected these cats will weigh?

    A   5 lb
    B   up to 5 lb
    C   3 lb
    D   5 kg

27   There is a spelling error in the fifth paragraph. Which word would have to be used to correct the error?

    A   weighting
    B   interested
    C   way
    D   matture

28 Which statement summarises the text?

    A   it describes a new breed of cat which scientists consider will
         end the problem of humans' allergies to cats
    B   it describes a new breed of cat which everyone agrees will
         solve the allergies some humans have to cats
    C   it describes an expensive new breed of cat which scientists
         believe will not cause allergies to humans, but about which
         animal organisations in the UK have concerns
    D   it describes an expensive new breed of cat developed in
         America and welcomed in the UK by the RSPCA and the asthma
         charity

29 What is the main purpose of the text?

    A   to bring new information to readers' attention
    B   to persuade readers to buy
    C   to amuse readers
    D   to describe the work of American scientists

Questions 30 to 34 relate to this advertisement

Porto Santo Lines, Madeira
Ferry : Lobo Marinho

**One-day cruise
Leaving Madeira
at 08:00**

**Arriving in Porto Santo
at 10:30**

Lobo Marinho leaving Madeira

Travel in style on the ferry "Lobo Marinho" and spend all day on the
island of Porto Santo where there are golden, sandy beaches, a
lively capital city and golf courses. Three-hour site seeing tours are
available.*

Arrive back in Madeira at 22:30.

Special offer between 8 March and 23 April – only
£45 per person return, including complimentary buffet dinner on
return journey.

Contact: Porto Santo Lines 291 228 994
* Please arrange with Porto Santo Lines at the time of booking

---

30   What is the length of the journey from Madeira to Porto Santo?

    A   2 hours

    B   2 ½ hours

    C   5 hours

    D   24 hours

31   What is the name of the ferry?

    A   Madeira

    B   Porto Santo

    C   Lobo Marinho

    D   Porto Santo Lines

32   What must be arranged at the time of booking?

    A   the return ticket

    B   site seeing tours

    C   the complimentary buffet

    D   playing golf

33   How much would two people pay for a return journey?

    A   £45

    B   £90

    C   £4.50

    D   £9

34   What is offered as extra during the special offer period?

    A   a buffet meal

    B   a reduced price ticket

    C   a complimentary buffet dinner on the return journey

    D   a free ticket for another person

Questions 35 to 40 relate to this letter

15 Tea Party Lane
MARCH
Cambridgeshire
CB2 6AW

madhatters@march.co.uk
01763 456289

Mrs H Lemington
Badgers' Brook Farm
CONDERLEY
Cambridgeshire
CB6 9HY

Dear Madam

Thank you for your recent enquiry concerning hiring hats for the ladies in your daughter's wedding party on 20th March.

We are pleased to enclose our price list and a cattalogue of some of the hats we have currently available.

Might we sugest that after you have had the opportunity to study the cattalogue, you might like to visit us so we can discuss your requirments. At that time you will have the opportunity to see a wider selection of our hats for all occasions.

Please telephone either myself or Maria Hattersley to make an appointment. We are both available on 3rd November and the 15th November.

We look forward to welcoming you.

Yours sincerely

Madelaine Hatter

Madelaine Hatter

Encs

35   What standard, essential, piece of information is missing from this letter?

    A   the telephone number of the recipient
    B   the date the letter was written
    C   the topic of the letter
    D   the title of the writer

36   The salutation is incorrect. What should it be?

    A   Dear Sir or Madam
    B   Dear Madame
    C   Dear Mrs Lemington
    D   Dear Mrs Lemmington

37   When is the wedding due to take place?

    A   2nd March
    B   3rd November
    C   20th March
    D   15th November

38   There is a spelling error in the second paragraph. Which word would need to be included in order to correct the error?

    A   ennclose
    B   catalogue
    C   currantely
    D   availabel

39   There are three spelling errors in the third paragraph. Which words would need to be included in order to correct the errors?

    A   sugesst; oportunnity; catalogue
    B   catalogue, requirements, occassions
    C   suggest, catalogue, requirements
    D   disscuss, requirmants, occassions

40   What would best describe the purpose of the letter?

    A   acknowledging a customer's enquiry and offering assitance
    B   offering assistance and making a firm appointment
    C   confirming an order and making an appointment
    D   acknowledging a customer's enquiry and sending a catalogue

END OF PAPER FOUR   END OF PAPER FOUR   END OF PAPER FOUR

Practice Multiple-choice Paper
suitable for:

Key Skills Level 1 Communication;
Level 1 Adult Literacy (Basic Skills); and
ESOL Skills for Life Level 1 Reading

Paper Five

YOU NEED
- This test paper.
- A pen.
- A pencil and eraser.
- An Answer Sheet.

You may NOT use a dictionary.
There are 40 questions on this paper. Try to answer ALL the questions.
When you have completed the questions you must check your answers,
then check them again.

YOU HAVE ONE HOUR TO FINISH THE PAPER

INSTRUCTIONS
- Make sure you write your name and today's date on the Answer Sheet. Use a pen to do this.
- Use a pencil to mark your answers so if you change your mind you can erase your choice and select another.
- Make sure that for each question you have only selected one answer. If you select more than one, the answer will not be marked.
- Read each question carefully before you select an answer.

Note for learners and tutors: This is a practice test that has been designed to closely resemble the questions and question styles of a 'live" paper.

Questions 1 to 9 relate to the text **Zoom Airways**

ZOOM AIRWAYS

Check our prices

You cannot do better

Get away for 7 days

One of the latest additions to our fleet

DESTINATIONS AND DESTINATION COSTS
(ALL FLIGHTS FROM BOURNEMOUTH)

Germany £88[1] 3* hotels with breakfast	Argentina £555[2] 4* hotels with breakfast	Brazil £545[4] 4* hotels with breakfast
Trinidad £530[3] 3* hotels	Portugal £155[1] 4* hotels with breakfast	Czech Republic £386[3] 3* hotels
Sweden £159[4] 3* hotels with breakfast	Finland £180[4] 3* hotels with breakfast	Mexico £425[2] 4* hotels with breakfast

[1] Travelling 1 July – 31 August 2008

[2] Travelling 1 May – 15 October 2008

[3] Travelling 18 August – 4 September 2008

[4] Travelling 26 June – 14 August 2008

Hotel rates are per person, based on two people sharing a room

Flights from other UK Regional Airports
Supplements
(Additional cost per person)

Durham and Tees Valley	Bristol	East Midlands	Manchester	Glasgow
£24	£8	£16	£21	£30

www.zoomairways.co.uk
ZoomAirways@flightpath.co.uk

Zoom Airways
16 Madeira Gardens
Bristol
SM14 5KL

1   If the **destination costs** were arranged in ascending price order, which destination would come **fourth**?

   A   Finland
   B   Portugal
   C   Czech Republic
   D   Sweden

2   Footnote number 4 relates to travel between 26 June and 14 August. How many destinations does this refer to?

   A   1
   B   2
   C   3
   D   4

3   If two people wanted to go to Brazil but lived in Glasgow, how much **extra** would they each have to pay?

   A   £24
   B   £18
   C   £30
   D   £21

4   If you wanted to go on holiday **anywhere** on 25th August. How many destinations could you select from?

   A   5
   B   6
   C   7
   D   8

5   Where is the office of Zoom Airways?

   A   Madeira
   B   Bristol
   C   Bournemouth
   D   Glasgow

6   Which is the **cheapest** destination?

   A   Mexico
   B   Germany
   C   Finland
   D   Portugal

7 How many 3* hotels include breakfast in the cost?

   A   4
   B   2
   C   3
   D   1

8 How many destinations offer one person 7 days, flying from Bournemouth, for less than a **total** price of £300?

   A   4
   B   3
   C   2
   D   1

9 What is the purpose of the document?

   A   to promote sales
   B   to promote destinations
   C   to list regional airports
   D   to advertise the addition of a new plane

Questions 10 to 16 relate to this text

BLOOMING PLANTS NURSERY

Care Leaflet Number 6 of 23
Using and Looking after Blooming Plants' Urns and Pots

To ensure the long life of your **Blooming Plants** urns and pots, we recommend:

- allowing adequate drainage

- useing good compost

- raising the pot off the ground.

Types of Container

Terracotta A weathered pot looks attractive. To speed up the aging process, cover the outside with a little yoghurt.

Wood A **Blooming Plants** container is made of hardwood but over time wood needs care. Treat every year with a wood preservative.

Stoneware The most hardwearing material. Clean with water and a soft cloth.

For further leaflets in this series visit www.bloomingplants.com

10   How many Care Leaflets are in the series?

     A   6
     B   23
     C   17
     D   16

11   Where does Blooming Plants recommend pots and urns should be placed?

     A   in a greenhouse
     B   on the soil
     C   off the ground
     D   near a water supply

12   What makes a terracotta pot age more quickly?

     A   standing in the rain
     B   covering with soil
     C   wiping with a soft cloth
     D   covering the outside with yoghurt

13   How often should someone use a preservative on a wooden container?

     A   each month
     B   every year
     C   every summer
     D   only in the winter

14   If someone wanted any more information, how could they get this?

     A   by visiting the company's website
     B   telephoning for a leaflet
     C   emailing Blooming Plants Nursery
     D   sending a fax to Blooming Plants Nursery

15   There is a spelling error in one of the bulleted points. Which word should be included to correct this error?

     A   alowing
     B   using
     C   raysing
     D   of

16   What is the main purpose of the leaflet?

    A   to advertise Blooming Plants' containers
    B   to get customers to write to the nursery with comments
    C   to sell plant containers
    D   to give advice about container gardening

Questions 17 to 21 relate to this table

JET-ESCAPE AIRWAYS
Flight Supplements from Regional Airport to Destinations

Regional Airport	Destination	Supplement*
Belfast	Palma	£49.00
Belfast	Faro	£49.00
Birmingham	Palma	£49.00
Bournemouth	Palma	£30.00
Bristol	Faro	£27.00
Cardiff	Palma	£34.00
City of Derby	Faro	£36.00
Durham Tees Valley	Palma	£55.00
Edinburgh	Faro	£57.00
Exeter	Faro	£27.00
Glasgow	Paris Orly	£62.00
Liverpool	Paris Orly	£48.00
Newcastle	Paris Orly	£60.00
Newcastle	Palma	£67.00
Norwich	Palma	£51.00
Norwich	Faro	£50.00
Stansted	Palma	£41.00
Stansted	Faro	£35.00
Stansted	Paris Orly	£33.00

* per person, return journey

17   Which regional airport charges the highest supplement?

    A   Palma
    B   Newcastle
    C   Glasgow
    D   Edinburgh

18   What is the destination, and from which airport, which has the most expensive supplement?

    A   Paris Orly from Glasgow
    B   Palma from Newcastle
    C   Faro from Norwich
    D   Paris Orly from Newcastle

19   Which airports fly to **both** Palma and Faro?

    A   Stansted and Belfast
    B   Belfast and Durham Tees Valley
    C   Belfast, Stansted and Norwich
    D   Newcastle and Norwich

20   How many regional airports are listed?

    A   19
    B   15
    C   16
    D   14

21   What would be the supplement cost for two people flying to Paris Orly from Stansted return?

    A   £33.00
    B   £60.00
    C   £66.00
    D   £122.00

Questions 22 to 26 relate to this text and charts/graphs A, B, C, D

GREENLINE TELEPHONE COMPANY

Bill Number: 57638/GFE   Tele No: 01357 342538
Bill Date: 15 September Total: £52.38
Bill Period: 16 July to 15 September

Destination	Number of Calls	Total length of calls
Portugal	12	1hr : 3mins : 12secs
Fleetwood	2	0hr : 24mins: 9secs
St Austell	6	0hr : 53mins : 27secs
Fair Isle	1	0hr : 16mins : 12secs
Scarborough	15	3hr : 52mins : 37secs
Folkestone	6	3hr : 54mins : 11secs
Mobile Phone	10	0hr : 7mins : 21secs

Payment of this account is NOW DUE. Please settle the account before 23 September
Payment Methods: Cheque made payable to *Greenline Telephone Company*
                              Online by visiting *www.greenlineteleco.co.uk*

A

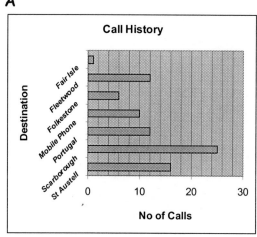

B

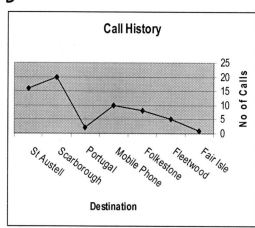

C

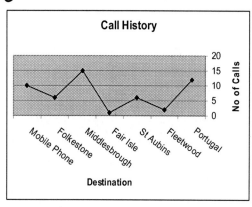

D

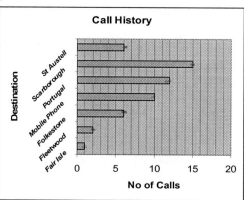

---

22 What is the bill date of the telephone account?

A 15 September
B 16 July
C 23 September
D 16 September

23 Where did the account holder telephone most often?

A Mobile Phone
B Portugal
C Scarborough
D Fair Isle

24 To which destination did the account holder talk the longest?

A Portugal
B Scarborough
C St Austell
D Folkestone

25 How many methods can the account holder use to pay the bill?

A 1
B 2
C 3
D 4

26 Which chart/graph accurately reflects the Destination of Number of Calls made by the account holder?

A A
B B
C C
D D

Questions 27 to 31 relate to this telephone message

WHISKERS AND WOOFS LUXURY HOTEL FOR CATS AND DOGS

TELEPHONE MESSAGE SHEET

From: Mr Seth Partridge   **To:** Amanda Berkley

Contact Details:
Tele Nos   (Home) 818198
(Work) 878787   Mobile No: 0797979469

Date: 17 March 2007

Mr Partridge wants to book in his two cats and his dog next month and wants you to confirm the cats can share a cabin.

I confirmed the booking from 7th to 12th April inclusive, but you will have to ring him to confirm the cabin arrangements for Twinkle and Harriet. His dog, Bob, has been assigned Cabin D14 for his stay.

I have checked and Cabin C24 is available for the two cats.

Please ring him either at his home number after 4.30 pm today or at work before 3 pm. You can ring his mobile between noon and 1 pm.

Carmina Stockbridge

27   What is the name of Mr Partridge's cats?

    A   Bob and Twinkle
    B   Harriet and Twinkle
    C   Twinkle and Harry
    D   Harriett and Carmina

28   For whom is the telephone message?

    A   Seth Partridge
    B   Harriet Partridge
    C   Carmina Stockbridge
    D   Amanda Berkley

29   Which statement is true in relation to the text?

    A   there is no double cabin available for the dates requested
    B   cabin D14 is available for the cats
    C   cabin C24 is available for the dates
    D   cabin C24 is available, but it is a single cabin

30   If the recipient of the message telephones the client at 7pm, which number should be dialled?

    A   818199
    B   878787
    C   0797979469
    D   818198

31   How many days will the pets be staying?

    A   4
    B   5
    C   6
    D   7

Questions 32 to 40 relate to this article

Romano Homes, Serbia	Line 1
Romano Homes' has created an exclusive development called Lime Grove, which has 1-bedroomed apartments and spacious 2-bedroomed apartments and penthouses in one of the prettiest resorts of Serbia.	
The long sandy beeches, just 1km from the Lime Grove development, are some of the best and most beautiful on the Serbian coast.	Line 5
The site is in a fortunate spot in the village of Barkavia. Walking for 5 minutes you will reach shops, cafes, restaurants, supermarkets and a modern private hospital. The location is surrounded by agricultural fields with no permission to build further homes or properties.	Line 10
Lime Grove apartments have been equipped with various luxury features to offer its residents a top-class life style.	
All the acommodation has private gardens reached through their outdoor pool area. There are generously-sized rooms with fitted wardrobes, open staircases, en-suite bathrooms, floor to ceiling patio doors, granite kitchen worktops, granite window and balcony sills and many more details which contribute to a feeling of luxury.	Line 15
There is a leisure outdoor pool and carefully landscaped garden areas and 24-hour security is provided on the site. A fully-equipped sauna and gym are located in the grounds.	Line 20
Prices start at £44,999 to £71,999.	
Contact Romano Homes at romanoinfo@serbia.com	

32 The second paragraph contains a spelling error. Which word would need to be included to correct this?

    A   beaches
    B   lime
    C   developement
    D   beutiful

33 How far from the development are the nearest shops?

    A   1 km
    B   a walk of five minutes
    C   5 km
    D   a walk of 1 minute

34 What do the window sills and the kitchen worktops have in common?

    A   they are painted black
    B   they are available in three colours
    C   they are granite
    D   they are a luxurious feature

35 There is a spelling error on **Line 13**. Which word would be needed to correct this error?

    A   accommodation
    B   privatte
    C   wreatched
    D   there

36 What is available 24 hours a day?

    A   the gym
    B   the outdoor pool
    C   the sauna
    D   site security

37 The word "contribute" is used in **Line 17**. Which alternative word could be used without altering the meaning of the text?

    A   donate
    B   add
    C   supply
    D   help

38   How can an interested reader contact the company?

   A   by telephone
   B   by email
   C   by logging onto the world wide web
   D   by fax

39   What is the purpose of the article?

   A   to provide interest in Serbia
   B   to advertise the area
   C   to give details of the apartments
   D   to encourage sales of the properties

40   What is the name of the development?

   A   Romano Homes
   B   Lime Gardens
   C   Lime Grove
   D   Barkavia

END OF PAPER FIVE   END OF PAPER FIVE   END OF PAPER FIVE

Practice Multiple-choice Paper
suitable for:

Key Skills Level 1 Communication;
Level 1 Adult Literacy (Basic Skills); and
ESOL Skills for Life Level 1 Reading

Paper Six

YOU NEED
- This test paper.
- A pen.
- A pencil and eraser.
- An Answer Sheet.

You may NOT use a dictionary.
There are 40 questions on this paper. Try to answer ALL the questions.
When you have completed the questions you must check your answers,
then check them again.

YOU HAVE ONE HOUR TO FINISH THE PAPER

INSTRUCTIONS
- Make sure you write your name and today's date on the Answer Sheet. Use a pen to do this.
- Use a pencil to mark your answers so if you change your mind you can erase your choice and select another.
- Make sure that for each question you have only selected one answer. If you select more than one, the answer will not be marked.
- Read each question carefully before you select an answer.

Note for learners and tutors: This is a practice test that has been designed to closely resemble the questions and question styles of a "live" paper.

Questions 1 to 10 relate to this text

BLACKPOOL TOWER	Line 1
Blackpool Tower, rising about the towns' skyline, is an impressive sight and is a world-famous Victorian landmark.	
The tower, which has recently been restored, appears as a lattice-work of red-coloured solid steel, but only from the ground. When you are traveling up to the top of its 518 feet in the lift, there seems to be very little steal between you and the view along the coast.	Line 5
At the top is the Walk of Faith, which is nothing other than a big pane of glass for a floor, giving a view of the ground some 400 feet below.	
In 1992, Blackpool Tower's lift was replaced with a new high speed model. This lift travels approximately 10,000 miles a year as it takes Blackpool's visitors 500 feet above sea level to the Towers' first observation platform.	Line 10
If you are not comfortable about heights, then a visit to the basement of the Tower is probably more to your liking.	
In this basement is an award-winning circus held several times daily and the show usually concludes with a spectacular dropping of the circus ring allowing floods of water to enter.	Line 15
There is also a spacious and richly-decorated dance hall with a fine floor and a absolutely wonderful Wurlitzer organ. Ballroom dancers have programmes in the afternoons and evenings.	Line 20
There are bars and tea bars and food and it's got an extensive aquarium with sea horses and giant turtles and a Jungle Jim's for the children with ball pools and scramble net's, rope swings and slides and more.	

1   Apostrophes have been used wrongly three times. In which lines do these errors occur?

   A   2, 10 and 23
   B   10, 12 and 22
   C   2, 12 and 23
   D   12, 21 and 23

2   There is a spelling error in **Line 5**. Which word would need to be included to correct the error?

   A   colored
   B   steal
   C   travelling
   D   travvelling

3 There is a spelling error in **Line 6**. Which word would need to be
   included to correct the error?

   A   their
   B   two
   C   steel
   D   betwene

4 How high is the tower?

   A   500 feet
   B   518 feet
   C   400 feet
   D   10,000 feet

5 How far is it estimated the tower lift travels a year?

   A   1,000 miles
   B   19,920 feet
   C   10,000 miles
   D   518 feet

6 What is the special feature at the top of the tower?

   A   it has one pane of glass for a window
   B   the floor is made of glass
   C   there is a circus ring
   D   ballroom dancing is held there

7 The word **concludes** is used in **Line 16**. What alternative word could
   be used without altering the meaning of the text?

   A   starts
   B   finish
   C   finishes
   D   decides

8 There is a grammatical error in **Line 18**. How should this line be
   corrected?

   A   There are also a spacious and richly-decorated dance hall with
       a fine floor and a
   B   There is also a spacious and richly-decorated dance halls with a
       fine floor and a
   C   They is also a spacious and richly-decorated dance hall with a
       fine floor and an
   D   There is also a spacious and richly-decorated dance hall with a
       fine floor and an

9 When can you take part in ballroom dancing?

    A   every day until 11 pm
    B   afternoons and evenings
    C   every evening
    D   mornings and evenings

10 What do you think is the main purpose of the text?

    A   to advertise the resort of Blackpool
    B   to advertise the circus and its unusual feature
    C   to celebrate the Tower's restoration
    D   to encourage visitors to the Tower

Questions 11 and 15 relate to these charts on blood donations

Chart A

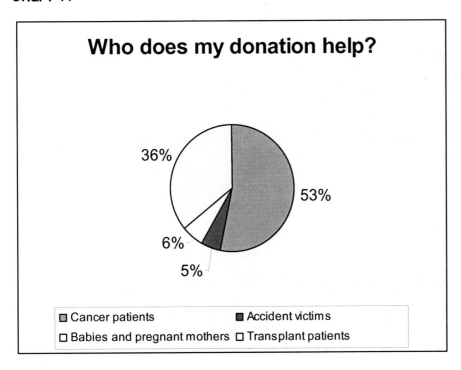

Who does my donation help?

36%

53%

6%

5%

▨ Cancer patients ▨ Accident victims
▢ Babies and pregnant mothers ▢ Transplant patients

Chart B

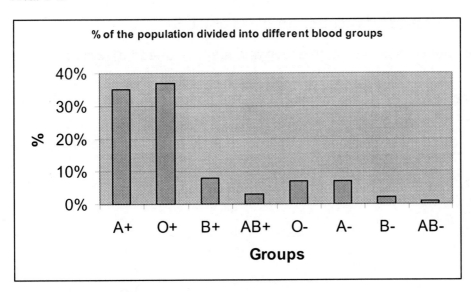

% of the population divided into different blood groups

A+ O+ B+ AB+ O- A- B- AB-

Groups

Questions 11 and 12 relate to **Chart A**

11 Which type of patient **most** benefits from blood donations?

   A Babies and pregnant mothers
   B Accident victims
   C Transplant patients
   D Cancer patients

12   Which type of patient receives blood transfusions the **least**?

    A   Transplant patients

    B   Babies

    C   Accident victims

    D   Cancer patients

Questions 13 to 15 relate to **Chart B**

13   What is the total number of blood groups shown on the chart?

    A   6

    B   8

    C   4

    D   5

14   Which blood group is the most common in the population?

    A   A+

    B   O+

    C   AB+

    D   A

15   Which is the accurate statement about blood group B+?

    A   it is the fourth most common group and slightly ahead of Group B

    B   there are fewer B+ group members of the population than Group A-

    C   it is the third most common group and slightly ahead of Group A

    D   Group B+ and B- are even, but lower than Group A+

Questions 16 to 22 relate to this letter

HIGH FLYING INSURANCE
COMPANY

Floor 5, Lightstock House,
NOTTINGHAM
NT3 17AF

Tele : 01743 445667
Highflying@balloon.com

17 December 2007

Mr I Hartman
Treetop Farm
Bowater Lane
ULVISTON
Cumbria   CB28 6GH

Life Policy Number 74658/HJI/1993
Outstanding Total £34.58

We have been advised by your bank branch that your Direct Debit instruction for the
above policy has been canselled.

If you wish to reinstate this policy please complete the Direct Debit form enclosed
and forward your check for the outstanding amount.   Upon receipt of the form and
your payment, we will reinstate the policy.

Yours sincerely

Lionel Ledley

Lionel Ledley
Customer Services Manager

Enc

16   What standard piece of information is missing from this letter?

   A   the date the letter was written
   B   the subject of the letter
   C   the salutation
   D   the complimentary close

17 There is a spelling error in the first paragraph of the letter. Which
   word would need to be included in order to correct the error?

   A   adviced
   B   Dirrect
   C   policie
   D   cancelled

18 How should the letter have begun?

   A   Dear Sir or Madam
   B   Dear Mrs Hartman
   C   Dear Mr Hartman
   D   Dear Mr I Hartman

19 The word **reinstate** is used in the second paragraph. Which
   alternative word could be used without altering the meaning of the
   sentence?

   A   restore
   B   cancel
   C   begin
   D   continue

20 What does the recipient need to do in order to reinstate their
   policy?

   A   telephone Mr Ledley
   B   complete the Direct Debit form and return it with the money
        owed
   C   complete the Direct Debit form and return it
   D   cend the money owed

21 There is a spelling error in the second paragraph of the letter.
   Which word would need to be included in order to correct the
   error?

   A   compleet
   B   foreward
   C   cheque
   D   reciept

22 Why does the abbreviation **Enc** appear at the end of the letter?

   A   to indicate it is the end of the letter
   B   because documents are enclosed with the letter
   C   to indicate an envelope needs to be addressed
   D   because the recipient must return some documents

Questions 23 to 29 relate to this text

STUDIO 7

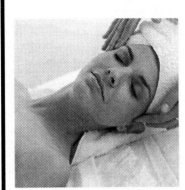

Ashton Road, Lymm,
Cheshire
01737 687687

Leaflet 6 of 10
Available from
Reception at Studio 7

Complimentary Therapies
(other therapies are available and are detailed in the remaining leaflets)

Reiki : Meaning "Universal Life Energy" 1 hour £20.00	The practitioner places their hands non-intrusively, in a sequence of positions which cover the whole body. The whole person is treated rather than specific symptoms.
Which conditions can Reiki help?	It is possible to heal at any level of being: physical, mental, emotional or spiritual.
Indian Head Massage 30 minutes £18.00	A soothing treatment, ideal for relaxation. A wonderful treatment to ease aching shoulders, neck, headaches and eyestrain. Aids insomnia, lack of concentration and tension headaches.
Thai Seated Massage 30 minutes £22.00	A relaxing treatment that will concentrate on the muscles and joints of the back, arms, head and neck, to leave you feeling lighter.
Bioenergiser Detox Spa 30 minutes £12 (course of 4 treatments £40.00)	A 30-minute foot spa treatment, which provides a feeling of well-being and relaxation, whilst at the same time cleaning and rebalancing your body by absorbing sodium ions and minerals. Your body's energy can be unbalanced by lack of fresh fruit and vegetables; together with little or no exercise, and stress. The treatment helps restore natural balance.

For further details on any treatment and to book an appointment ring
Dan on 01737 687688

23   Which therapy has the lowest cost **per hour**?

    A   Thai Seated Massage
    B   Detox Spa
    C   Indian Head Massage
    D   Reiki

24   What is the purpose of the document?

    A   to promote healthy living
    B   to describe all the therapies the Studio offers
    C   to describe some therapies and encourage enquiries and bookings
    D   to take bookings by telephone

25   The word **specific** is used in the Reiki text. Which alternative word could be used without altering the meaning of the text?

    A   exact
    B   alternative
    C   unnamed
    D   problem

26   How many reasons are given for a body's energy being unbalanced in the Detox Spa text?

    A   2
    B   3
    C   4
    D   5

27   How many information leaflets are available from the Studio?

    A   2
    B   6
    C   8
    D   10

28   Why would someone ring Dan?

    A   to ask for the other leaflets in the set
    B   to either get details of other treatments or make an appointment
    C   to ask directions to the Studio
    D   because the number for the Studio is engaged

29   Which treatment would be best for someone who suffered from headaches and had an aching neck?

    A   Thai Seated Massage
    B   Reiki
    C   Indian Head Massage
    D   Detox Spa

Questions 30 to 32 relate to this document

PETS SAFE AT HOME

To   Anne Aldridge, Finance Clerk

From Sandra Sooty, Customer Care Manager

Date 11/11/07

Re   Cheque for Mrs M Hartley

Would you please let me have **today** a cheque, to the value of £3.00, made payable to Mrs M Hartley.

I am writing to this customer and wish to enclose the cheque with the letter. Please ring my secretary Jane on Extension 353 so she can collect it urgently.

Thank you

Sandra

30   This is an example of what kind of business document?

    A   letter
    B   memorandum
    C   report
    D   notice

31   The date has been incorrectly written. How should it appear?

    A   11/11/2007
    B   11 November 07
    C   11 November 2007
    D   11 Nov 07

32   Whose telephone number is 353?

    A   Anne Aldridge
    B   Sandra Sooty
    C   Jane Sooty
    D   Sandra's secretary Jane

Questions 33 to 40 relate to this text about **Pluto**

PLUTO IS NO LONGER A PLANET	Line 1
On 24 August 2006 the Institute of Technology in California announced that the Planet Pluto, discovered in 1930 by the American Clyde Tombaugh, was to be redefined as a "dwarf planet".	
Scientists agreed that in order to be classified as a planet, one thing it must be is a celestial body which must orbit around a star whilst not itself being a star.	Line 5
A spokesman for the ITC said that scientists are finding more planets in our solar system and some are larger than Pluto. The number of planets in our solar system has increased in recent years and they are now seperated into two categories - planets and dwarf planets.	Line 10
The decision to strip Pluto of its status as a planet has meant that school text books need to be rewritten to reflect the fact their are now only eight planets in our solar system: Mercury, Venus, Earth, Mars, Jupiter, Saturn, Uranus and Neptune.	
	Line 15

33   What do the initials **ITC** stand for in relation to this article?

    A   Institute of Travelling and Communication
    B   Independent Technology of California
    C   Institute of Technology
    D   Institute of Technology in California

34   How many categories of planets are there?

    A   5
    B   8
    C   3
    D   2

35   How many planets are there **now** in our solar system, according to the article?

    A   9
    B   8
    C   7
    D   14

36 What is the significance for schools in Pluto being no longer classed at a planet?

   A   lessons which mention the solar system will have to be stopped
   B   schools will no longer be able to mention Pluto
   C   text books will have to be rewritten to reflect the change in the number of planets
   D   text books will have to list planets and dwarf planets separately

37 **Line 6** includes the phrase "which must orbit around a star". Which alternative word could be used instead of the words **orbit around** without altering the meaning of the text?

   A   pass
   B   loop
   C   travel
   D   circle

38 There is a spelling error on **Line 9**. Which word would need to be included in order to correct the error?

   A   soler
   B   resent
   C   increesed
   D   separated

39 There is a spelling error on **Line 12**. Which word would need to be included in order to correct the error?

   A   knead
   B   reflecct
   C   there
   D   eigt

40 How can the text best be described?

   A   factual
   B   interesting
   C   argumentative
   D   opinion

END OF PAPER SIX   END OF PAPER SIX   END OF PAPER SIX

Practice Multiple-choice Paper suitable for:

Key Skills Level 1 Communication; Level 1 Adult Literacy (Basic Skills); and ESOL Skills for Life Level 1 Reading

Paper Seven

YOU NEED
- This test paper.
- A pen.
- A pencil and eraser.
- An Answer Sheet.

You may NOT use a dictionary.
There are 40 questions on this paper. Try to answer ALL the questions.
When you have completed the questions you must check your answers,
then check them again.

YOU HAVE ONE HOUR TO FINISH THE PAPER

INSTRUCTIONS
- Make sure you write your name and today's date on the Answer Sheet. Use a pen to do this.
- Use a pencil to mark your answers so if you change your mind you can erase your choice and select another.
- Make sure that for each question you have only selected one answer. If you select more than one, the answer will not be marked.
- Read each question carefully before you select an answer.

Note for learners and tutors: This is a practice test that has been designed to closely resemble the questions and question styles of a "live" paper.

Questions 1 to 6 relate to the text **Safer Mobile Phones?**

SAFER MOBILE PHONES?	
Mobile phone theft could be elliminnated by a system which makes stolen handsets useless.	Line 1
As soon as the telephone is stolen a self-destruct message can be sent to it and this wipes all its contents and permanently locks the keys so no further calls can be made. If, at any point, thieves try to replace the Sim card, the handset will emit an ear-piercing scream.	Line 5
Every year in Britain around 700,000 phones are stolen. This costs consumers around £390 million.	
Recent figures reveal that muggings have risen as thiefs target mobile phones and iPod music players. Mobile phones are thought to be a factor in almost half teenage robberies.	Line 10
With the knew phone, if it is stolen, the owner contacts the company, which sends a self-destruct message to the mobile. This wipes its memory and locks the keys. It also triggers an alarm which will activate if there is any attempt made to remove the Sim card.	Line 15

1   There is a spelling error in **Line 1**. Which word would need to be included in order to correct the error?

    A   elimminated
    B   eliminated
    C   thefft
    D   systtem

2   The word **emit** is used in **Line 6**. Which alternative word could be used without altering the meaning of the text?

    A   send
    B   creating
    C   produce
    D   product

3   There is a spelling error in **Line 9**. Which word would need to be included in order to correct the error?

    A   Resent
    B   reveel
    C   thieves
    D   targett

4   There is a spelling error in **Line 12**. Which word would need to be included in order to correct the error?

   A   new
   B   contracts
   C   companie
   D   ownar

5   How can the article best be described?

   A   opinion
   B   polite
   C   informative
   D   confusing

6   Which of these statements is correct when related to the text?

   A   Around seventy thousand mobile phones are stolen each year in Britain.
   B   Mobile phones are stolen in almost half teenage robberies and it costs the owners around seven hundred million pounds a year.
   C   Britain's consumers lose around £390 a year as a result of mobile phone thefts when almost seven hundred thousand phones are stolen annually.
   D   The new type of mobile phone will reduce phone thefts in Britain from 390 million a year.

Questions 7 to 13 relate to this text

Forth Road Bridge This bridge is situated 9 miles west of Edinburgh and spans the Firth of Forth between South Queensferry and North Queensferry.	Line 1
Construction began on this suspension bridge in 1958 with the work undertaken by three of the largest construction firms in Britain.	Line 5
Queen Elizabeth II opened the bridge on the 4th September 1964. At the time it was the longest bridge in the world outside the USA.	
The project cost £11.5 million, with a further £8 million needed for the approach roads. Crossing the bridge in a motor vehicle is subject to the payment of tolls for motorised traffic, although it is free for pedestrians.	Line 10
Traffic is carried on four lanes and frequently exceeds 70,000 vehicles per day and long queues are regular at peak-time travel times.	
The bridge is nearly 1828m long and its towers are over 150m high. The cables which suspend the road and walkway are 5.9cm in diameter. The total length of wire in the whole bridge is 49,280 km.	Line 15

7 The word **spans** appears in **Line 2**. Which alternative word or phrase could be used without altering the meaning of the text?

A length
B extends beyond
C extends over
D covers

8 How can the text best be described?

A a mix of fact and opinion
B factual
C complaining
D contradictory

9 How many firms were involved in building the bridge?

A 1
B 3
C 4
D 6

10 How much did the **bridge** cost to build?

A £11 million
B £8 million
C £11.5 million
D £19.5 million

11 The word **exceeds** appears on **Line 11**. Which alternative word or phrase could be used without altering the meaning of the text?

A beat
B goes above
C extends
D increases

12 How many lanes does the road across the bridge include?

A 1
B 2
C 3
D 4

13 To what does the figure 49,280 km relate?

  A   the length of the bridge
  B   the height of the towers
  C   the length of the road
  D   the length of cabling in the bridge

Questions 14 to 23 relate to this advertisement

SHIPSHAPE TRAVEL COMPANY

NEW YEAR OFFERS◊

Ports of Call	Ship	Dates of Departure	No. of Nights	Cost per person*
Fly UK to Barbados, St Kitts, Dominica, Trinidad, Grenada, Barbados, Fly to UK	Ocean Village	17 February 24 March 11 June	15	£1059
Fly UK to Barbados, St Lucia, St Maarten, Madeira, Gibraltar, Sardinia, Naples, Corfu, Athens Fly to UK	Calypso Islands	17 April 30 May 10 July 8 August	23	£2499
Harwich, Oslo, Copenhagen, Stockholm, Helsinki, Tallinn, Harwich	Jewel of the Northern Seas	16 April 25 May 20 June 16 July	12	£799
Southampton, Vigo, Lisbon, Barcelona, Florence/Pisa, Rome, Gibraltar, Southampton	Anadora	3 May 18 June 14 July 25 August	19	£1698
Fly UK to San Juan, Barbados, Antigua, St. Maarten, Grenada, Aruba, San Juan Fly to UK	The Caribbean Star	17 February 23 March 27 April 9 June	15	£1459
Fly UK to Palma, Palermo, Naples, Marseille, Barcelona, Palma Fly to UK	Destiny	17 May 28 June 26 July 25August 20 September	14	£796

◊   offers available for booking from midnight 23 December until mid-day 5 January
* prices are based on 2 people sharing an outside cabin with balcony.

SHIPSHAPE TRAVEL COMPANY
www.shipshapecruising.co.uk (for details of our company)
To make a booking: Freephone 08015 676468

14   What is the purpose of the document?

    A   to encourage people to go on cruising holidays
    B   to give details of how successful the company is
    C   to advertise special offers and encourage bookings
    D   to promote year-round holiday cruises

15   What is the first day and time when someone could book a cruise shown in the text?

    A   midnight 5 January
    B   mid-day on 23 December
    C   mid-day on 5 January
    D   midnight on 23 December

16   What is included in the **Cost per person**?

    A   an outside cabin on the ship with two people sharing it
    B   an outside cabin on the ship, with a balcony, and two people sharing the cabin
    C   an inside cabin on the ship with two people sharing it
    D   an inside cabin on the ship, with a balcony, and two people sharing the cabin

17   How many ways can someone contact the company to make a booking?

    A   1
    B   2
    C   3
    D   4

18   Why is the company's website address included?

    A   to help people make a booking
    B   to make sure everyone who books visits the website first
    C   to enable the company to send confirmation of booking via email
    D   to enable people to find out information on the company

19   How many departure dates has The Caribbean Star?

    A   4
    B   10
    C   12
    D   15

20   If a traveller wanted to visit Barbados, which cruise liners visit the island?

   A   Ocean Village and The Caribbean Star
   B   The Caribbean Star and Destiny
   C   Ocean Village, The Caribbean Star and Calypso Islands
   D   The Caribbean Star and Calypso Islands

21   How many holidays include flights from the UK then return flights to the UK?

   A   2
   B   4
   C   5
   D   6

22   Which ship has the cheapest cruise?

   A   Destiny
   B   Jewel of the Northern Seas
   C   Anadora
   D   Ocean Village

23   If the **Ships** were arranged in alphabetical order, which would come second on the list?

   A   The Caribbean Star
   B   Destiny
   C   Calypso Islands
   D   Jewel of the Northern Seas

Questions 24 and 25 relate to the table below and graphs A, B, C and D which reflect sales of kilos of fruit in the summer months in Better Buy Supermarket

Month	Oranges	Grapes	Bananas
June	45000	26000	36000
July	36000	34000	39000
August	38000	29000	27000

Graph A

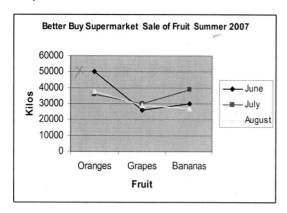

Graph B

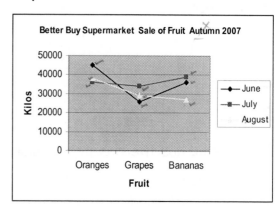

Graph C

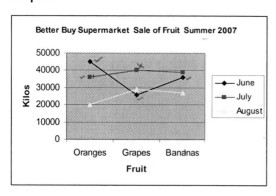

Graph D

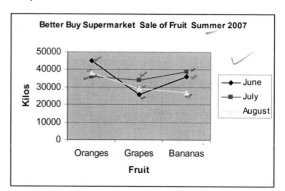

24 Which graph accurately represents the sales figures shown in the table?

A   A
B   B
C   C
D   D

25 Which fruit and month reflect the **highest** sales?

A   Grapes in June
B   Oranges in August
C   Oranges in June
D   Bananas in July

Questions 26 to 32 relate to this letter

RAPID COMMUNICATION NETWORK

Correspondence Centre
DURHAM
DH28 5GG

6 October 2007

Mr J Heaton
16 Collingwood Close
FERRYHILL
Co Durham   DH19 5LJ   Line 5

Dear Sir

<u>Account Number 17648FB</u>

Thankyou for contacting Rapid Communication Network (RCN). As a valued
eBilling customer you may be interested to know that in order to continue with
this service, you may need to update your eBilling details.   Line 10

You can do this by logging on to www.rcn.com/youraccount and following these
steps :

1 Log in with your user name and password
2 Click **Your profile** tab
3 Click **Accounts**   Line 15
4 Click **Edit Account** to change your details.

We are also here if you encounter any problems. Please do not hesitate to email
us at rcn@problems.co.uk at any time.

Yours sincerley

Jillian O Sweeney

Jillian O Sweeney   Line 20
Customer Service Director

---

26   The salutation is incorrect. How should this be corrected?

   A   Dear Sir or Madam
   B   Dear Mr J Heaton
   C   Dear Sirs
   D   Dear Mr Heaton

27   There is an error on **Line 8**. How should this be corrected?

    A   Thank you
    B   contracting
    C   Comunnication
    D   valuable

28   What is the purpose of this letter?

    A   to persuade the customer to become an eBilling customer
    B   to ask the customer to contact them for information
    C   to tell the customer they have done something wrong and how to put it right
    D   to inform and offer guidance

29   The word **encounter** is used in **Line 17**. What alternative word, or phrase, could be used without altering the meaning of the text?

    A   agree with
    B   come across
    C   entertain
    D   mark

30   There is an error in the complimentary close. How should this be corrected?

    A   Yours truly
    B   Yours faithfully
    C   Yours sincerely
    D   Kind regards

31   What job has the writer of the letter?

    A   Consumer Service Director
    B   Customer Service Director
    C   Customer Manager
    D   Customer Accounts Service Director

32   What is the purpose of the **emboldened** text in the numbered paragraphs?

    A   there is no purpose it just looks attractive
    B   to help the customer read the letter
    C   to give clear details of the steps involved when on the website
    D   to encourage the customer to use the website

Questions 33 to 40 relate to this text

FROM 1ˢᵀ JULY 2007

ENGLAND HAS BEEN SMOKEFREE

IN WORK PLACES AND PUBLIC PLACES

Almost all enclosed public spaces and workplaces became smokefree in England in 2007. These places include restaurants, offices, factories, bars and public transport. If a work vehicle, for instance a delivery van, is used by more than one person, it to must be smokefree.

All smokefree businesses must display appropriate signs, and this includes company vehicles.

If you want any spare signs then order via the website www.smokefreeengland.co.uk

Support for the Campaign

- 78% of adults support the smokefree law and this includes 90% of non-smokers and 47% of smokers
- Second-hand smoke is harmful to health and this is supported by 57% of people
- 75% of the public, half of whom are smokers, believe that going smokefree will have a positive effect on everyone's health.

The Benefits

It is thought that as a result of smokefree public and work places thousands of lives could be saved in the next ten years.

It is believed that this ban will result in 70% of smokers quitting the habit.

33   What is the main purpose of the text?

    A   to encourage business to take part in the Smokefree campaign
    B   to persuade people to stop smoking
    C   to provide important information
    D   to advertise a non-smoking website

34   When did England become smokefree?

    A   31 July 2007
    B   30 June 2007
    C   1 July 2007
    D   1 June 2007

35   There is a spelling mistake in the third line of the first paragraph.
Which word would correct this error?

    A   instence
    B   deliverie
    C   vehical
    D   too

36   Of the 78% of adults who support the smokefree law, what
percentage are non-smokers?

    A   47%
    B   90%
    C   75%
    D   70%

37   What do 57% of people believe?

    A   the smokefree law will not work
    B   the smokefree law will have a positive effect on people's health
    C   second-hand smoke is harmful to health
    D   second-hand smoke has no effect on people's health

38   What percentage of people is it believed will stop smoking as a
result of this law?

    A   57%
    B   73%
    C   90%
    D   70%

39 Under what circumstances must a work vehicle become a smokefree area?

    A   when it is used as public transport
    B   when it is used every day
    C   when it is used by more than one person
    D   when it is a delivery van

40 How can someone get spare smokefree signs?

    A   visit the website named in the text
    B   write to the Government
    C   write to the Department of Health
    D   photocopy their existing signs

END OF PAPER SEVEN END OF PAPER SEVEN

END OF PAPER SEVEN

Practice Multiple-choice Paper
suitable for:

Key Skills Level 1 Communication;
Level 1 Adult Literacy (Basic Skills); and
ESOL Skills for Life Level 1 Reading

Paper Eight

YOU NEED
- This test paper.
- A pen.
- A pencil and eraser.
- An Answer Sheet.

You may NOT use a dictionary.
There are 40 questions on this paper. Try to answer ALL the questions.
When you have completed the questions you must check your answers,
then check them again.

YOU HAVE ONE HOUR TO FINISH THE PAPER

INSTRUCTIONS
- Make sure you write your name and today's date on the Answer Sheet. Use a pen to do this.
- Use a pencil to mark your answers so if you change your mind you can erase your choice and select another.
- Make sure that for each question you have only selected one answer. If you select more than one, the answer will not be marked.
- Read each question carefully before you select an answer.

Note for learners and tutors: This is a practice test that has been designed to closely resemble the questions and question styles of a "live" paper.

Questions 1 to 10 relate to this text

<u>SOLAR PANELS ON SALE IN HIGH STREET SHOPS ARE THE LATEST CONSUMER DEMAND</u>	Line 1
As energy bills soar and the UK experiences increasing temperatures, householders are finding solar panels on sale in electric stores next to TVs, washing machines and personal computers.	
Buying a solar panel, however, is not cheap. Installing one in a typical 3-4 bedroomed house will cost up to £9,000.	Line 5
This system is able to reduce energy bills by up to fifty percent.	
Evidence from other European countries suggests the installation adds to a properties value. At present the systems have a 25-year guarantee, although it is expected they will last longer than that. Some parts, however, may need replacing after 10 years.	Line 10
Solar panels will not require planning permission and retailers believe they will compete with conservatories and loft conversions as the most popular home improvement.	
Traditional fuels are being exhausted and experts say that petrol and oil will be gone in fewer than 40 years; natural gas in 60 years and coal in 200 years. The sun transmits more energy to the earths surface in just one hour than mankind uses in a year, so capturing a small percentage of this will help solve the worlds' energy problems.	Line 15

1   What is the main purpose of the text?

    A   to make consumers think about climate change
    B   to inform readers about a new product and its benefits
    C   to tell readers where to buy the new product
    D   to promote an alternative means of heating the home

2   The word **soar** appears in **Line 2**. What alternative word could be used without altering the meaning?

    A   fly
    B   rise
    C   drop
    D   circle

3   Where can solar panels be purchased?

    A   in high street shops
    B   in other European countries
    C   in electric stores
    D   in home improvement stores

4   The word **reduce** appears in **Line 7**. What alternative word could be used without altering the meaning?

    A   promise
    B   meet
    C   cut
    D   increase

5   In **Line 8** there is a punctuation error. Which word would have to be inserted to correct the error?

    A   properties'
    B   suggests'
    C   suggest's
    D   property's

6   For how many years is a solar panel guaranteed?

    A   10
    B   a lifetime
    C   25
    D   40

7   The word **compete** appears in **Line 11**. What does this mean?

    A   having a solar panel will become as popular as having a conservatory or a loft conversion
    B   solar panels will be more expensive than conservatories
    C   solar panels are better than having conservatories
    D   more people will have loft conversions than solar panels

8   What kind of fuel is likely to have disappeared in 200 years' time?

    A   oil
    B   coal
    C   natural gas
    D   petrol

9   There is a punctuation error in **Line 15**. Which word would have to be inserted in order to correct the error?

    A   uses'

    B   use's

    C   earths'

    D   earth's

10   There is a punctuation error in **Line 16**. Which word would have to be inserted in order to correct the error?

    A   worlds

    B   problems'

    C   world's

    D   problem's

Questions 11 to 20 relate to **Global Warming**

GLOBAL WARMING	
Global Warming is encourageing farmers to produce a range of Mediterranean-style crops.	Line 1
Vineyards, olive groves, chillis, tea, nuts are flourishing because of soaring temperatures. Livestock such as ostriches are permnent residents at Darren Copeland's Hill Top Farm in Stroud, Gloucestershire.	Line 5
The range of crops means that farms in southern England are becoming similar to parts of the Mediterranean, Africa and the Middle East.	
As Britains weather heats, some producers are discovering an advantage to global warming. In southern England it is creating a new climate suitable for growing all sorts of exotics. One such grower, Patrick Fforbes, is building a business based on his belief that temperatures will get even hotter. He is growing almonds, pecans, sharon fruits, apricots, walnuts and olives at his farm near Honiton in Devon.	Line 10

11   There is a spelling error on **Line 1**. Which word should be used to correct this error?

    A   encouraging

    B   farrmers

    C   two

    D   product

12   There is a punctuation error on **Line 8**. Which word should be used to correct this error?

    A   Britains'

    B   Britain's

    C   heat's

    D   producer's

13   The word **flourishing** is used on **Line 3**. What alternative word or phrase could be used without altering the meaning of the text?

    A   thriving

    B   increasing

    C   up-and-coming

    D   promising

14   There is a spelling error on **Line 4**. Which word should be used to correct this error?

    A   tempratures

    B   ostrickes

    C   permanent

    D   residence

15   Where is the farm that has ostriches?

    A   Devon

    B   Honiton

    C   Stroud

    D   Gloucester

16   What is the name of Mr Copeland's farm?

    A   Copeland's Farm

    B   Top Farm

    C   Hill Top Farm

    D   Stroud Farm

17   Where does Mr Fforbes farm?

    A   Stroud, Gloucestershire

    B   Africa

    C   Honiton, Cornwall

    D   Honiton, Devon

18   How many types of crop does Mr Fforbes grow?

   A   2
   B   4
   C   6
   D   5

19   The phrase "based on his belief that" appears on **Line 11**. Which alternative phrase could be used without changing the meaning of the text?

   A   as a result of
   B   because he knows that
   C   because research shows that
   D   because he is of the opinion that

20   Which of the following best summarises the text?

   A   All Britain's farmers are able to grow more exotic crops as a result of worldwide global warming.
   B   Global warming has caused Britain's farmers to grow crops associated with the Middle East, rather than traditional oats, barley and wheat.
   C   In years to come British farmers will be growing crops associated with hotter countries because of global warming.
   D   The world's weather is increasing in temperature, and farmers in Britain are now able to grow crops, and breed livestock, which are more usually associated with the countries of Africa, the Middle East and the Mediterranean.

Questions 21 to 30 relate to this text

FITNESS STUDIO AND POOL
www.fitnessstudioandpool.co.uk
Members Classes 14 April - 16 May

MONDAY	TUESDAY	WEDNESDAY	THURSDAY	FRIDAY	COMMENCING 14 APRIL
Spin Express 0715 - 0745 (SS)	Groove FX 1000 - 1045 (S1)	Spin Express 0715 - 0745 (SS)	Tone Express 0800 - 0830 (MB)	Groove FX 0730 - 0815 (S1)	
Yoga 0930 - 1015 (MB)	Spin Express 1300 - 1345 (SS)	Pilates 1045 - 1130 (S2)	Salsa 0930 - 1015 (S3)	Abs Blast 1035 - 1000 (S2)	
Abs Blast 1035 - 1100 (S1)	AquaRobics 1430 - 1515 (SP)	Abs Blast 1200 - 1225 (S3)	Tone Express 1230 - 1300 (S1)	AquaRobics 1530 - 1615 (SP)	
Tone Express 1230 - 1300 (S1)	ASL* 1515 - 1600 (SP)	Tone Express 1230 - 1300 (MB)	AquaRobics 1530 - 1615 (SP)	Salsa 1730 - 1815 (SS)	
Yoga 1430 - 1515 (MB)	Spin Climb 1730 - 1815 (SS)	Yoga 1400 - 1445 (MB)	Yoga 1700 - 1745 (MB)	Pilates 1830 - 1915 (MB)	At Fitness Studio and Pool it's always time to begin you're next class and commence a fitness programme
Salsa 1830 - 1915 (S1)	Pilates 1800 - 1915 (MB)	Salsa 1530 - 1615 (S1)	Spin Climb 1800 - 1845 (SS)	Pilates 1900 - 1945 (S3)	
Studio Step 1845 - 1945 (S3)	Salsa 1800 - 1900 (S3)	ASL* 1600 - 1645 (SP)	AquaRobics 1900 - 2000 (SP)	AquaRobics 1900 - 1945 (SP)	A

*ASL Adult Swimming Lessons (maximum of 20 persons each session)

Key :

SS	Spin Studio	
S1	Studio 1	
S2	Studio 2	
S3	Studio 3	
SP	Small Pool	
MB	Mind and Body Studio	

Fitness Studio and Pool
Opening Hours

Mon - Thursday	**06:30 – 22:00**
Friday	**06:30 – 21:00**
Saturday and Sunday	**08:00 – 19:00**

Telephone : 01672 882991

The Studio : St Cuthbert's Lane : Pinge : Dorset
Other branches in Exeter, Colchester, Norwich, Derby, Lincoln Preston

21 There is a punctuation error in the **third line** of the heading. How should this be corrected?

A Members' Classes 14 April - 16 May
B Member's Classes' 14 April - 16 May
C Members Class's 14 April - 16 May
D Members Class'es 14 April - 16 May

22 On how many days are **Tone Express** classes held?

A 1
B 2
C 3
D 4

23 Which of these statements is true in relation to the timetabled classes?

A Spin Climb and Studio Step have the same number of classes and there are five classes of Salsa and Pilates.
B Yoga classes occur most in the week and the Pilates classes occur only in the Mornings.
C There is only one class of Studio Step, but AquaRobics has five classes a week.
D The Groove FX classes occur in the mornings and evenings on three of the Days.

24 In which area is the **Pilates** class most usually held?

A Studio 2
B Spin Studio
C Studio 3
D Mind and Body Studio

25 On which day is the Salsa class at 17:30 and the AquaRobics two hours earlier?

A Thursday
B Friday
C Tuesday
D Monday

26   How many times a week does the timetable show the Mind and Body
     Studio in use?

     A   2
     B   4
     C   6
     D   8

27   Where is this branch of the Fitness Studio and Pool situated?

     A   Exeter
     B   Pinge
     C   Lincoln
     D   Derby

28   Including this branch, how many branches of Fitness Studio and Pool
     are there?

     A   5
     B   6
     C   7
     D   8

29   There is a spelling/punctuation error in the text at **A**. Which word
     would need to be included in order to correct this error?

     A   beggin
     B   its
     C   your
     D   program

30   What is the maximum number of people who can be included in the
     Adult Swimming Lessons?

     A   5
     B   10
     C   15
     D   20

Question 31 relates to the charts A, B, C and D, below, in relation to the following table

Destination	Regional Airport	Supplements
Palma	Belfast	£49.00
Palma	Birmingham	£49.00
Palma	Bournemouth	£30.00
Palma	Stansted	£37.00
Palma	Norwich	£53.00

31 Which of the following charts accurately illustrates the information shown in the table?

A   A
B   B
C   C
D   D

A

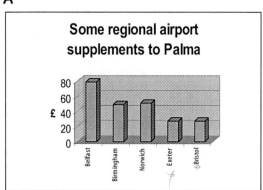

B

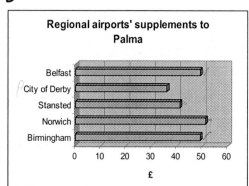

C

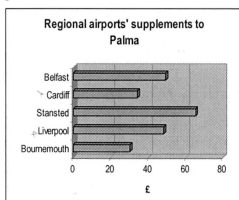

D

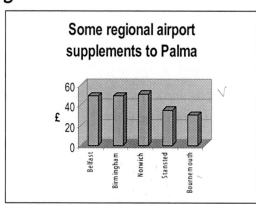

Questions 32 to 34 relate to this document

Carter's
Stay Fast Nail Varnish
High Gloss, Sparkly Colour Range

25% off

(whilst stocks last)

EVETTE AND COXON

6 High Row, Darlington,
Co Durham

evettandcoxon@beautyinc.com

Bring this coupon to claim your 25% discount valid from 16/6 until 20/7

32   What is the purpose of this document?

   A   an advertisement for nail varnish

   B   an advertisement for a product and a discount voucher for a store

   C   a discount voucher for Evette and Coxon

   D   a promotional document

33   Which of these statement is true in relation to the text?

   A   Anyone going to Evette and Coxon between 16 June and 20 July will receive 25% off their purchase of any Carter's Nail Varnish.

   B   Whilst stocks last between 16 May and 20 June customers can get 25% off a selected range of Carter's Nail Varnish.

   C   The High Gloss, Sparkly Colour Range of Carter's Nail Varnish is subject to a 35% discount during the period 16 June to 21 July in every branch of Evette and Coxon.

   D   Whilst stocks of Carter's High Gloss, Sparkly Colour Nail Varnish last in Evette and Coxon in Darlington, customers producing this voucher will get a 24% discount between 16 June and 20 July.

34   There is an error in the company's email address. How should this error be amended?

   A   eveteandcoxon@beautyinc.com
   B   yvetteandcoxon@beautyinc.com
   C   evetteandcoxon@beautyinc.com
   D   evvetteandcoxon@beautyinc.com

Questions 35 to 40 relate to **Nuisance Telephone Calls**

NUISANCE TELEPHONE CALLS	Line 1
Nuisance telephone calls can be offensive, threatening or simply very annoying.	
Some nuisance callers may dial your number at random. Others may know you. Whichever group they fall into, remember **you are in control**.	Line 5
Keep calm Most nuisance callers gain pleasure by getting a response from you. So keep calm and put the receiver down, walk away from the phone and after a few minutes return and hang up the phone.	
Don't give your number when you answer the phone at home just say "hello". If a caller asks "What number is this?" ask what number they are trying to contact. Make sure callers identify themselves first. If you have a telephone answering machine, do not put your number in the answering message.	Line 10
British Telecom is there to help you if you experience malicious calls. Call their Nuisance Call Advisors free of charge any time of the day or night on **Freefone 0800 661 441**. They will offer advice on the most suitable action to take. In some cases they can also work with the Police to trace your calls.	Line 15

35   The phrase **at random** is used in **Line 4**. What would be an alternative phrase or word which could be included without altering the meaning the text?

   A   by chance
   B   hit and miss
   C   accidentally
   D   by intention

36   What should you not say when answering the telephone?

   A   your name
   B   your telephone number
   C   "hello"
   D   your name and number

37 What would be a recommended response to a caller's request "What is your number?"

    A   "That's none of your business."
    B   "I don't want to tell you that."
    C   "What number are you ringing?"
    D   "Why do you want to know?"

38 What advice does the article give relating to answering machine messages?

    A   say you are not at home
    B   don't include your telephone number
    C   make the caller speak first
    D   never leave it switched on

39 Who, or what, can be reached on Freefone 0800 661 441?

    A   British Telecom
    B   the Police
    C   nuisance call network
    D   British Telecom's Nuisance Call Advisors

40 What is the purpose of the article?

    A   to frighten readers
    B   to reassure readers
    C   to advertise British Telecom services
    D   to give an opinion

END OF PAPER EIGHT   END OF PAPER EIGHT

END OF PAPER EIGHT

Practice Multiple-choice Paper
suitable for:

Key Skills Level 1 Communication;
Level 1 Adult Literacy (Basic Skills); and
ESOL Skills for Life Level 1 Reading

Paper Nine

YOU NEED
- This test paper.
- A pen.
- A pencil and eraser.
- An Answer Sheet.

You may NOT use a dictionary.
There are 40 questions on this paper. Try to answer ALL the questions.
When you have completed the questions you must check your answers,
then check them again.

YOU HAVE ONE HOUR TO FINISH THE PAPER

INSTRUCTIONS
- Make sure you write your name and today's date on the Answer Sheet. Use a pen to do this.
- Use a pencil to mark your answers so if you change your mind you can erase your choice and select another.
- Make sure that for each question you have only selected one answer. If you select more than one, the answer will not be marked.
- Read each question carefully before you select an answer.

Note for learners and tutors: This is a practice test that has been designed to closely resemble the questions and question styles of a "live" paper.

Questions 1 to 6 relate to this document that appeared in a magazine

I CAN,   CAN YOU?

To celebrate the Midshire County Council's promotion to encourage more people to recycle their cans and other recyclable material, we are giving away a folding bike made from recycled material.

- Recycling cans helps to cut down the amount of rubbish being sent to landfill
- Recycling helps reduce the harmful gasses produced when makeing new products

To win the bike, simply answer the following question:

Q **How many tons off cans were recycled last year through the Household Waste Recycling Centres and Kerb-It recycling collection scheme?**

Send your entries, together with your name, address and telephone number to our address which you will find on Page 2 of this magazine.

1   How can this article **best** be described?

   A   an advertisement
   B   informative
   C   a competition
   D   factual

2   Who is giving away the prize?

   A   Waste Recycling Centres
   B   Kerb-It Recycling Centre
   C   The Midshire Recycling Centre
   D   Midshire County Council

3   The prize is a bike. If this was written in full, which would be the correct spelling?

   A   bycycle
   B   bicycle
   C   bycicle
   D   bisickle

4   There is a spelling error in one of the two bullet points. How should this error be corrected?

   A   recycleing
   B   ammount
   C   harmfull
   D   making

5   There is a spelling error in the **Question text**. How should this be corrected?

   A   tunns
   B   of
   C   threw
   D   Waist

6   How can the reader find details of where to send their entry?

   A   in the local telephone book
   B   on the back page of the magazine
   C   on page 2 of the magazine
   D   on page 12 of the magazine

Questions 7 to 16 relate to this letter

PACK AND GO HOLIDAYS LTD

Acorn house   RIVERSIDE   DUBLIN   DB2 7jl

www.packandgo.com   **01538 264265**

23 March 2007

Mr and Mrs K Birch
15 Liffey View
Dublin
DB7 5HJ

Dear Mr Birch

Thankyou for your enquiry about skiing holidays. We are pleased to summarise details of the main skiing resorts of Europe and hope this is of interest to you.

<u>Lillehammer, Norway</u>   160km from Oslo Airport

There is said to be no better place to take the children than this enchanting Norse wonderland. Scandinavia has a reputation as an inexpensive and accessible recreational resort with low-cost airlines putting this unspoilt part of Europe at the top of their charter flight list.

Lillehammer was home to the 1994 Olympics.

<u>Les Arcs, France</u>   140km from Geneva Airport

France is a most popular ski destination. The French Alps are so well designed that once you have picked a holiday base, many resorts are accessible just by hopping in a chairlift to make the journey across the valley. Book early for Christmas week. There's a nightly torch-lit descent and firework display.

<u>Chamonix, France</u> 88km from Geneva Airport

This is a world famous resort. It is sophisticated and is the perfect choice for serious skiers. Don't miss the 30-minute helicopter tour taking in the breathtaking Mont Blanc.

<u>Bormio, Italy</u>   200km from Milan-Malpensa and Linate Airports

Built by the Romans as a spa town, Bromio is beautiful. One of a cluster of resorts off the beaten ski path. Popular with British skiers, it retains an air of exclusivity lost in some other, more mainstream resorts. There is low-key nightlife and quaint restaurants. Check out the hot springs: they are a tonic for aching muscles and cold toes!

If you require further information, please do not hesitate to contact us. You can email one of our specialist winter holiday staff directly on candice@packandgo.co.uk or telephone us during our opening hours of Monday to Saturday 09:00 – 18:00. We look forward to booking your skiing holiday in the near future.

Yours faithfully

Jennifer Morrison

Jennifer Morrison
Agency Manager

7   The salutation is incorrect. How should this have been written?

    A   Dear Mr K Birch
    B   Dear Mrs K Birch
    C   Dear Mr and Mrs K Birch
    D   Dear Mr and Mrs Birch

8   What would be a suitable heading for the letter?

    A   Skiing Holiday Information
    B   Skiing Holiday Booking - Winter 2007
    C   Winter 2007 Skiing Holiday availability
    D   A guide to Europe's Winter Holiday Destinations

9   There is an error in the first paragraph of the letter. How should this be corrected?

    A   Thank you
    B   inquirie
    C   Wer'e
    D   Sumarrise

10 What is the purpose of the letter?

    A   to confirm a holiday booking
    B   to enclose skiing holiday brochures
    C   to respond to a customer's enquiry asking for details of some European skiing resorts
    D   to quote holiday prices to a customer

11 If the customers want to travel **the least distance** from the airport to their resort, which destination would they select?

    A   Lillhammer
    B   Les Arcs
    C   Chamonix
    D   Bormio

12 The term candice@packandgo.co.uk is an example of what?

    A   a website
    B   an email address
    C   a fax address
    D   freephone contact details

13 Which countries' ski resorts are mentioned in the letter?

    A   France and Switzerland

    B   Norway, France and Switzerland

    C   Italy and France

    D   Italy, Norway and France

14 For holidays in which resort are people advised to book early for Christmas?

    A   Lillehammer

    B   Les Arcs

    C   Chamonix

    D   Bormio

15 Which resort was formerly a spa town?

    A   Les Arcs

    B   Bormio

    C   Chamonix

    D   Lillehammer

16 Who wrote the letter?

    A   Pack and Travel Holidays Ltd

    B   Jennifer Morris

    C   Jennifer Morrison of Pack and Travel Holidays Ltd

    D   Jennifer Morrison of Pack and Go Holidays Ltd

Questions 17 to 24 relate to this text

MAIL PRICES : UK

The formats

Letter This includes postcards, letters and most greeting cards, up to 100g and no thicker than 5mm.

Large Letter This new format includes larger, or thicker, greeting card, A4-sized envelopes, CDs and DVDs in cases, under 750g and no thicker than 25mm.

Packet Anything longer, wider or thicker than a Large Letter, e.g. catalogues and video tapes.

Item	Weight (grams)	First Class	Second Class
Letter	0-100g	32p	23p
Large Letter	0-100g	44p	37p
	101-250g	65p	55p
	251-500g	90p	75p
	501-750g	131p	109p
Packet	0-100g	100p	84p
	101-250g	127p	109p
	251-500g	170p	139p
	501-750g	220p	177p
	751-1000g	270p	212p
	1001-1250g	474p	*
	Additional 250g or part thereof	+85p	

* Items heavier than 1000g cannot be sent Second Class

ADDRESS YOUR ENVELOPE CORRECTLY

- ⊠ **Always** use the correct address and correct postcode
- ⊠ **Write** the address clearly
- ⊠ **Don't** use bold fonts or very thick pens and never italics
- ⊠ **Print** the address so it's lined up on the **left**
- ⊠ **Don't** add the country in the address on mail originating in the UK
- ⊠ **When** posting abroad, always add the destination country, in English, on the last line of the address
- ⊠ **Don't** leave large gaps between the address lines, or between the address and the postcode.

FOLD YOUR A4 LETTERS IN HALF
AND SAVE MONEY BY SENDING THEM
IN A SMALLER ENVELOPE

17 How many formats of mail are mentioned in the text?

    A   2
    B   3
    C   4
    D   5

18 What is the purpose of the text?

    A   to advertise services
    B   to give an opinion
    C   to give facts
    D   to promote the Post Office

19 If you were posting two CDs to a friend, which format of post would you have to use?

    A   Letter
    B   Large Letter
    C   Packet
    D   Parcel

20 You want to post a Packet weighing 1005g. Which format will you have to use?

    A   Packet, second class
    B   Large Letter, first class
    C   Packet, first class
    D   Large letter, second class

21 You want to send a friend a birthday present that the Post Office classes as a Packet. It weighs 1600g. How much will you have to pay **extra** to the charge of 474p?

    A   85p
    B   185p
    C   559p
    D   170p

22 If you are writing an envelope to send to Norway, where would you put the country on the envelope?

    A   on the first line of the address
    B   on the top left of the envelope
    C   on the last line of the address
    D   on the back of the envelope

23 The word **originating** appears in the fifth bullet point. What alternative word could be used without altering the meaning of the text or the sentence?

    A   starting from
    B   beginning
    C   invented
    D   created

24 What is the tone of the text?

    A   argumentative
    B   humorous
    C   informative and factual
    D   opinion and informative

Questions 25 to 30 relate to this document

To	Vivian Corbett	
From	Stanley Hopkins	
Date	14 November 2007	
Re	XXXXXXX	

Further to your email requesting the Council's "Stay Safe" contact numbers, I have pleasure in listing these.

Title	Number*	Details
Community Safety	467266	24 hours
Neighbourhood Wardens	455590	7am - 11pm
Fire and Rescue	341290	24 hours
Victim Support	456290	24 hours
Racial Equality	355638	11am - 10pm
Drug and Alcohol Team	414142	7am - 6pm
Neighbourhood Watch	466566	24 hours

* each number has the area code 01464

If you require further information, please contact me again.

Stanley Hopkins

25 What type of business document is this?

    A   a business letter
    B   a notice
    C   a memorandum
    D   a report

26 What should the writer insert on the line **Re**, to reflect the content
of the document?

A   Your email
B   Contact numbers
C   Your request for information
D   Stay Safe Contact Numbers

27 If the **Title** column was arranged in alphabetical order, which entry
would come third?

A   Neighbourhood Watch
B   Neighbourhood Wardens
C   Drug and Alcohol Team
D   Fire and Rescue

28 If the **Title** column was arranged in alphabetical order, which entry
would come fifth?

A   Fire and Rescue
B   Neighbourhood Wardens
C   Neighbourhood Watch
D   Racial Equality

29 How many of the services are available for more than 12 hours a
day?

A   4
B   5
C   6
D   all of them

30 If someone was dialing the Victim Support line, what number would
they dial?

A   456290 01464
B   01446 456920
C   01464 456290
D   456092

Question 31 relates to this table of product sales and the charts A, B, C and D

Nourishing Oil Cosmetics plc

Product Sales

Product	Value of Sales (last month) £
Ginger Lotion 50ml	1,240.00
Ginger Lotion 200ml	1,520.00
Ginger Gel	890.00
Aloe Vera Gel 50ml	2,300.00
Aloe Vera Shampoo 50ml	450.00
Aloe Vera Conditional 40ml	600.00

Chart A

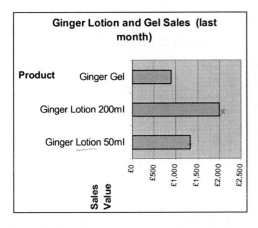

Chart B

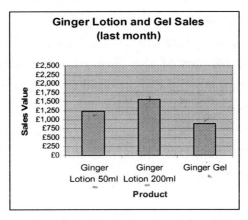

Chart C

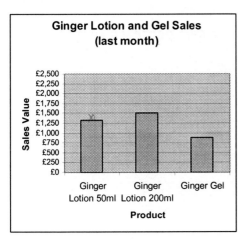

Chart D

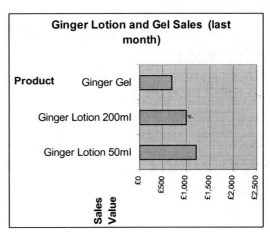

31 Nourishing Cosmetics plc has calculated its sales of Ginger products last month. These are shown in the table.

Which chart accurately illustrates the sales as shown in the table?

A A

B B

C C

D D

Questions 32 to 34 relate to spelling, grammar and punctuation

32 Which of the following sentences uses correct spelling, grammar and apostrophes?

A The owners of the High Flying Insurance Company is arranging two Christmas Lunchs' in the towns' Robin Hood Hotel.

B The owners' of the High Flying Insurance Company are arranging two Christmas Lunch in the town's Robin Hood Hotel.

C The owners of the High Flying Insurance Company are arranging too Christmas Lunches in the towns Robin Hood Hotel.

D The owners of the High Flying Insurance Company are arranging two Christmas Lunches in the town's Robin Hood Hotel.

33 Which of the following sentences uses correct spelling, grammar and apostrophes?

A Mad Hatter's is a hat making company with two partners who're both female.

B Mad Hatters is a hat making companie with too partners' whor'e both female

C Mad Hatters is a hat making company with two partners who're both female.

D Mad Hatters' is a hat making company with two partners' who'are both female.

34 Which one of the following sentences uses correct spelling, grammar and apostrophes?

    A   Shipshape Travel Company have forty special offers' for the months' of July and August. They're waiting for your call.

    B   Shipshape Travel Company has forrty special offer's for the months of July and August. Their' waiting for your call.

    C   Shipshape Travel Company have forty special offers' for the months' of July and August. They're waiting for you're call.

    D   Shipshape Travel Company has forty special offers for the months of July and August. They're waiting for your call.

Questions 35 to 40 relate to the text **Pavement Parking**

PAVEMENT PARKING	Line 1
The Borough of Midshire is urging car owners to avoid parking on pavements.	
The problems created by on-street parking are increasing and Midshire has many streets, especially in Puddlebarn Village and Hopley Village, where residents have no alternative to on-street parking.	Line 5
Terry Jones of Midshire Councils Environment Department says, "Parking on pavements affects pedestrians, especially the elderly, the disabled and those with a visual problem. Those with mobility problems and people with prams and pushchairs can also be affected."	
One of the outcomes of obstructing the pavements is to force people to walk into the road, which can be dangerous where the street is narrow with alot of traffic using the highway.	Line 10
Parking on pavements also causes damage to the flagstones and the kerbs and repairing these is expensive and will result in higher taxes for residents in Midshire Borough.	Line 15

35 Which two villages are named in the article?

    A   Puddleduck and Midshire

    B   Hopley and Puddleton

    C   Puddlebarn and Hopeley

    D   Hopley and Puddlebarn

36 There is a punctuation error on **Line 6**. How should this be corrected?

    A   Jone's

    B   Jones'

    C   Council's

    D   Councils'

37 The word **obstructing** is used in **Line 10**. What alternative word could be used without altering the meaning of the text?

A   clearing
B   blocking
C   avoiding
D   joining

38 What do people do which is dangerous when they come across a vehicle on a pavement?

A   squeeze past
B   cross the road
C   fall into the road
D   walk into the road

39 There is a spelling error in **Line 12**. How should this be corrected?

A   a lot
B   allot
C   useing
D   hyway

40 Why might the taxes increase for residents in Midshire Borough?

A   because money will be spent towing away cars parked on pavements
B   because money will be spent repairing damaged roads
C   because money will be spent repairing damaged pavements
D   because the Council will fine owners of cars parked on pavements

END OF PAPER NINE   END OF PAPER NINE   END OF PAPER NINE

Practice Multiple-choice Paper
suitable for:

Key Skills Level 1 Communication;
Level 1 Adult Literacy (Basic Skills); and
ESOL Skills for Life Level 1 Reading

Paper Ten

YOU NEED
- This test paper.
- A pen.
- A pencil and eraser.
- An Answer Sheet.

You may NOT use a dictionary.

There are 40 questions on this paper. Try to answer ALL the questions.

When you have completed the questions you must check your answers, then check them again.

YOU HAVE ONE HOUR TO FINISH THE PAPER

INSTRUCTIONS
- Make sure you write your name and today's date on the Answer Sheet. Use a pen to do this.
- Use a pencil to mark your answers so if you change your mind you can erase your choice and select another.
- Make sure that for each question you have only selected one answer. If you select more than one, the answer will not be marked.
- Read each question carefully before you select an answer.

Note for learners and tutors: This is a practice test that has been designed to closely resemble the questions and question styles of a "live" paper.

Questions 1 to 6 relate to the text **Ginger Lotion**

GINGER LOTION

Nourishing and Intensive

Available from
Nourishing Oil Cosmetics plc
17 Sandhurst Road
Elvington
YORK YO30 2PW
01904 564 567

Ginger Oil helps to:

- reduce the appearance of all scars (new and old)
- keep skin moisturised and elastic so reduces the appearance of uneven skin tone
- provide lubrication so prevents stretch marks
- replace skin's natural oils removed by extreme weather conditions (heat and cold)
- provide a hand and cuticle lotion
- firm and smooth the body when used as a bath oil.

Available in 50ml and 200ml bottles

50ml	£10.99
200ml	£16.99
Postage and packing	£4.50 (up to two items)
	£3.00 (three to five items)

Allow up to 14 working days for delivery

DON'T DELAY

ORDER TODAY

WHILST STOCKS OF THIS POPULAR PRODUCT REMAIN

1   Who sells this product?

    A   Sandhurst plc
    B   Nourishing and Intensive plc
    C   Ginger Lotion
    D   Nourishing Oil Cosmetics plc

2   What does the product claim to do to old scars?

    A   moisturize them
    B   reduce their appearance
    C   make them more firm
    D   make them disappear

3   Why would someone choose to use the product as a bath oil?

    A   because it replaces natural oils lost in bath water
    B   because it evens out skin tones
    C   because it moisturizes hands and feet
    D   because it firms and smoothes the body

4   What is the minimum number of items someone would have to buy in order to only spend £3.00 on postage and packing?

    A   3
    B   4
    C   5
    D   6

5   What is said to be the effect on the skin of hot and cold weather conditions?

    A   it causes uneven skin tone
    B   it makes skin rough
    C   it removes natural oils from the skin
    D   the skin is less elastic

6   After placing an order, how many days should a purchaser allow before expecting the goods to arrive?

    A   14
    B   up to 14
    C   up to 14 working days
    D   13 working days

Question 7 refers to the table below and charts A, B, C and D that reflect how Midshire Council spent its income

MIDSHIRE COUNCIL SPENDING 2006 – 2007

Service	£m
Environmental Services	23
Cultural Services	15
Highways and Transport	43
Social Services	204
Education	410

Chart A

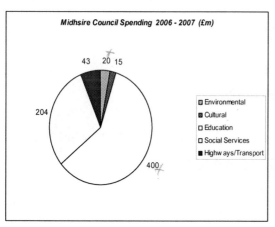

Chart B

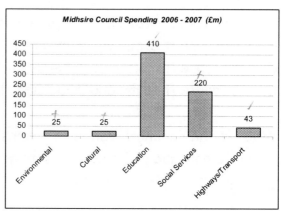

Chart C

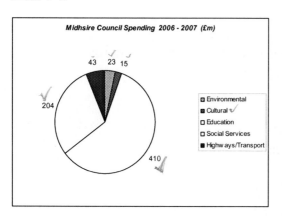

Chart D

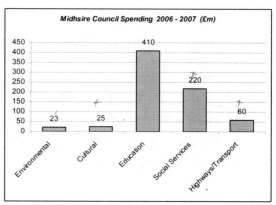

7   Which chart accurately illustrates the spending shown in the table?

A   A
B   B
C   C
D   D

Questions 8 to 12 relate to the text **Keeping the Roads Clear in Winter**

KEEPING THE ROADS CLEAR IN WINTER	Line 1
In the deep, midwinter, whilst most of the country sleeps, a dedicated team of workers make sure our main roads are clear and safe for our journeys.	
Beginning in October, gritters are on call to deal with the worst weather as thats the month the ground frosts usually begin.	Line 5
Once the weather forecasters say ground frost is on its way, overnight gritters carry out pre-salting of the countries' highways. Most Councils have such up-to-date equiptment they know where ice will form so the gritters can target the areas which are most in need.	
Throughout the winter months the ice prediction systems are monitored 24 hours a day to make sure the main roads are kept clear.	Line 10

8   How can the text best be described?

  A   interesting
  B   factual
  C   persuasive
  D   opinion

9   There is a punctuation error in **Line 5**. How should this be corrected?

  A   thats'
  B   that's
  C   frost's
  D   frosts'

10   There is a punctuation error in **Line 7**. How should this be corrected?

  A   gritter's
  B   gritters'
  C   country's
  D   countries

11 There is a spelling error in **Line 8**. How should this be corrected?

    A   equippment

    B   equipment

    C   no

    D   were

12 Why are the ice prediction systems monitored?

    A   to make sure they are working properly

    B   so information can be given about weather forecasts

    C   so no ice will form on the roads

    D   to make sure the roads are kept clear

Questions 13 to 17 relate to this table concerning library books

BOOKWORM LENDING LIBRARY

Books borrowed between 8 March and 14 August 2007

Times Borrowed	Author	Title
16	Polly Peacock	Fine Feathers
3	Harry Harper	Stamp Collectors in the 21st Century
18	Poppy Derwent	Views from Coniston Water
25	Isla White	The History of the Solent
14	Carla Shore	Cooking with Olive Oil
9	James Blenkinsop	The Glass Company
12	Erin Winters	The Four Seasons
26	Rose White	How to Pass Key Skills Tests
10	Amelia Fellowes	Shoes through the Centuries
3	Jack Pheasant	Keeping Poultry
21	Craig Weston	Touring the Channel Islands by Boat

13 If the authors' names were placed in alphabetical order of surname, which author would come second on the list?

    A   Harry Harper

    B   Amelia Fellowes

    C   Poppy Derwent

    D   Jack Pheasant

14 Which book has been the most popular during the period?

   A   How to Pass Key Skills Tests
   B   The history of the Solent
   C   Views from Coniston Water
   D   Cooking with Olive Oil

15 How many books have been borrowed **fewer than** 10 times in the period?

   A   1
   B   2
   C   3
   D   4

16 The library decides to sell those books that have not been borrowed 15 times or more. How many books will it offer for sale?

   A   3
   B   3
   C   5
   D   6

17 If you were to arrange the authors whose names begin with the letter **W**, into alphabetical order, what would be the correct order?

   A   White R; White I; Weston C; Winters R
   B   Winters R; White I; White R; Weston C
   C   Weston C; White I; White R; Winters R
   D   White I; White R; Winters R; Weston C

Questions 18 to 29 relate to this business letter

PRIMARY COLOURS INTERIOR DESIGNS

Unit 15 Todmorton Industrial Park

BELFAST BL12 7GG   01722 667467

20/09/07

Mr K Finch
Clayton Farm
Badger Lane
DUNMURRY

Dear Mr Finch

Following our designers visit to your home on 16 September to discuss redecorating the ground floor rooms of your farmhouse, we are pleased to give below our recommendations.

Study:		Dining Room:	
Walls	Soft sand	Walls	Lemon Ice
Doors (2)	Brownstone	Doors (2)	Lemon Fizz

Front Parlour:		Rear Parlour:	
Walls	Pale Terracotta	Walls	Pale Terracotta
Door (2)	Warm Terracotta	Doors (2)	Light Terracotta

Kitchen:		Utility Room:	
Walls	Water	Walls	Mint Julep
Doors (3)	Mint Crisp	Doors (2)	Mint Crisp

Laundry:	
Walls	China Blue
Doors (3)	Sarong

All woodwork, other than doors, to be brilliant white. All ceilings to be soft white.

Maura O'Sullivan, the designer, would like to visit you again to discuss this scheme in more detail and make arrangements for the work to begin. After you have had time to consider these proposals would you please telephone her on 01722 877468 to make an apointment. She will be on annual leave week commencing 8 October, returning on 17 October during which time her telephone will only take messages.

We look forward to being of further service to you.

Yours truly

Peter Painter

Peter Painter
Senior Partner

18 The letter is dated, but how should the date have been written?

  A 20 October '07
  B 20 September '07
  C 20 September 2007
  D 20 October 2007

19 Which company is Mr Finch dealing with?

  A Primary Colours
  B Primary Colours Interior Designs
  C Primary Paints Interior Designs
  D Primary Designs

20 There is a punctuation error in the first paragraph of the letter. Which word should be used to correct this error?

  A designers'
  B designer's
  C rooms'
  D recommendation's

21 How many doors are to be painted?

  A 10
  B 12
  C 14
  D 16

22 What colour will the paintwork and ceiling be painted?

  A Mint Crisp
  B Water
  C Soft White
  D Warm Terracotta

23 When did the designer call on the customer?

  A 20 September
  B 16 October
  C 18 September
  D 16 September

24 The complimentary close is incorrect. What should this be?

   A   Yours faithfully
   B   Your sincerely
   C   Yours sincerely
   D   Yours Sincerely

25 Who wrote the letter?

   A   Peter Painter
   B   Keith Painter
   C   Peter Finch
   D   Keith Finch

26 What is the name of the designer?

   A   Maria Sullivan
   B   Maura Sullivan
   C   Maura O'Sulivvan
   D   Maura O'Sullivan

27 There is a spelling error in the third paragraph. Which word should be used to correct this error?

   A   skeem
   B   arangements
   C   appointment
   D   comenncing

28 If the client rings the designer on 11 October, what will happen?

   A   the telephone will not be answered as the designer is on holiday
   B   the designer will ring him back later that day
   C   the client will have to contact the designer the following day
   D   he will not be able to speak to the designer, just leave a message

29 How can the purpose of the letter best be described?

   A   to give information and offer further help
   B   to request information
   C   to confirm information
   D   to give details of holiday plans

Questions 30 to 40 relate to this text

YOUR GUIDE TO WALKING IN THE COUNTRYSIDE

The Lundy Island, lying off the coast of North Devon, has some of the most beautiful countryside in Britain and is home to a wide range of plants and animals.

Guided Walks

Why not join one of the Island's guided walks and explore the countryside with experts? Walks cover the whole of the island and are led by a team of enthusiastic and knowledgeable volunteers, supported by stewards who make sure everyone is safe.

Walk Grades

EASY
Country walk suitable for most levels of fitness. Short walks, mainly on surfaced paths or pavements.

MEDIUM
Country walks suitable for people of average fitness. Comfortable walking on non-flat surfaces, avoiding strenuous climbs. Boots are essential.

HARD
Requires a good level of fitness. Walks with steep or strenuous climbs or rough moorland. Boots essential.

LONG
Requires a good level of fitness. Typical country walk which is suitable for people who can manage distance (over 8 miles) but want to avoid steeper terrain or climbs. Boots essential.

Distance and Duration of Walks

Alongside each walk we advertise* is the distance that will be covered and the approximate time the walk is expected to take. The timing of the walk is given as a guideline only. The pace depends on the fitness and number of people in the group and the weather conditions. The leader will adapt the pace to suit the slowest participant. All walks are circular unless otherwise stated.

* details of the organized walks, recommended month by month, are available from the Tourist Information Centre, Bideford, Devon.

THE COUNTRYSIDE CODE
- Be safe : plan ahead
- Read and follow signs
- Leave gates closed
- Protect plans and animals by taking your litter home
- Keep dogs under close control and supervision
- **Consider other people, especially those who live in the countryside**

30   Where is Lundy Island situated?

    A   off the south coast of Devon
    B   off the north coast of Cornwall
    C   off the north coast of Devon
    D   near Dorset

31   What is the purpose of the text?

    A   to advertise walks on Lundy and encourage participation
    B   to advertise the Tourist Information Centre
    C   to advise readers about the countryside code
    D   to encourage holiday makers to Lundy

32   How many grades of walks are described?

    A   1
    B   2
    C   3
    D   4

33   For how many of the walks are boots regarded as essential footwear?

    A   2
    B   3
    C   1
    D   all of them

34   Where can someone obtain details of the walks?

    A   from the Tourist Information Centre in Lundy
    B   from a steward
    C   from a resident of Lundy
    D   from the Tourist Information Centre in Bideford

35   What grade of walk would involve 10 miles of walking?

    A   easy
    B   long
    C   hard
    D   medium

36 Who leads each walking team?

    A   a walking enthusiast

    B   a knowledgeable volunteer

    C   a volunteer who is enthusiastic and knowledgeable

    D   a ranger who is knowledgeable

37 The text states that "all walks are circular unless otherwise stated". What does this mean?

    A   the walkers don't need a compass because they walk in circles

    B   the walk will begin and end in the same place

    C   walkers will walk in straight lines, one behind the other

    D   walkers are expected to draw circles on the ground

38 What is the importance of the slowest member in a walking group?

    A   the slowest walker will set off before other group members

    B   the leader will walk with the slowest person

    C   the slowest person will finish the walk last

    D   the leader will walk to the pace of the slowest person

39 How many grades of walk require a person to have a good level of fitness?

    A   1

    B   2

    C   3

    D   4

40 What are walkers asked to do with gates?

    A   close them

    B   walk round them

    C   climb over them

    D   leave them open

END OF PAPER TEN   END OF PAPER TEN   END OF PAPER TEN

Practice Multiple-choice Paper
suitable for:

Key Skills Level 1 Communication;
Level 1 Adult Literacy (Basic Skills); and
ESOL Skills for Life Level 1 Reading

Paper Eleven

YOU NEED
- This test paper.
- A pen.
- A pencil and eraser.
- An Answer Sheet.

You may NOT use a dictionary.
There are 40 questions on this paper. Try to answer ALL the questions.
When you have completed the questions you must check your answers,
then check them again.

YOU HAVE ONE HOUR TO FINISH THE PAPER

INSTRUCTIONS
- Make sure you write your name and today's date on the Answer Sheet. Use a pen to do this.
- Use a pencil to mark your answers so if you change your mind you can erase your choice and select another.
- Make sure that for each question you have only selected one answer. If you select more than one, the answer will not be marked.
- Read each question carefully before you select an answer.

Note for learners and tutors: This is a practice test that has been designed to closely resemble the questions and question styles of a "live" paper.

Questions 1 to 6 relate to this article **The Changing Weather of the United Kingdom**

THE CHANGING WEATHER OF THE UNITED KINGDOM	Line 1
On 16 October 1987 southern England woke up to what has since been called "the Great Storm". It resulted in the felling of 15 million trees and a cross-Channel ferry blew onto a beech.	
We live in a part of the world which has a climate not associated with hurricanes. The UK is rarely too hot, rarely too cold and certainly does not often see winds like the 122 mph wind which occurred in 1987. However, if the warning about climate change is to be believed, the UK is going to have to get used to more weather of this kind.	Line 5
In 2087, the centenary of the "Great Storm", our grandchildren and great-grandchildren will be living in a very different place to today's green and pleasant land.	
Current forecasts are based on computer models which work on complicated calculations and can be turned into forecasts for decades and even centuries ahead. Few people bothered with long-term climate forecasting in 1987; it was assumed the weather would remain unchanged. There was, at that time, some talk of an Ice Age, although even then some scientists began to worry that the effect of discharging billions of tons of carbon dioxide into the air would cause temperatures to rise rather than fall.	Line 10
	Line 15
Children of later this 21st century might be amused by tales of regular snowfall and the moans about soggy English summers. If the forecasters are to be believed, these two things could become a thing of the past in this century.	

1   There is a spelling error in **Line 3**. How should this be corrected?

    A   resullted
    B   milion
    C   Chanell
    D   beach

2   How can this text best be described?

    A   persuasive
    B   opinion
    C   humorous
    D   frightening

3   In 1987 how strong was the wind?

    A   very strong
    B   gale force
    C   hurricane force at 122 mph
    D   hurricane force

4   The word **discharging** appears in **Line 14**. What alternative word could be used without altering the meaning of the text?

  A   releasing
  B   entering
  C   creating
  D   throwing

5   The word **soggy** appears in **Line 17**. What alternative word could be used without altering the meaning of the text?

  A   long
  B   short
  C   cold
  D   wet

6   What is thought to be likely to happen as we put more and more carbon dioxide into the air?

  A   temperatures will fall
  B   floods will happen
  C   the winters will be longer
  D   temperatures will rise

Questions 7 to 12 relate to this article

AGE FOR DRIVING
SOLO COULD BE
RAISED TO 18

The Government has agreed to consider plans to raise the minnimum	Line 1
driving age to 18 in an attempt to reduce road accidents and deaths	
which are caused by young drivers.	
The scheme is to be called "graduated driving licence" and learner	
drivers will have to spend at least 12 months on their L-plates, which	Line 5
means they will have to drive under supervision. Although this would	
apply to learners of any age it has the effect of increasing the	
minimum age for a full licence from 17 to 18.	
The idea has been supported by key road safety groups and the	
Association of British Insurers who as welcome the proposal as a	Line 10
positive move to cut the death toll on UK roads.	
It is believed that more an 1,000 people a year – a third of them	
drivers – are killed in crashes involving a driver aged 17 to 25.	
The Government will set out details of the proposal in the winter of	
2007.	Line 15

7   There is a spelling error in **Line 1**. Which word should be added to
     correct this error?

    A   Goverment
    B   agrede
    C   concider
    D   minimum

8   What will the new scheme be called?

    A   raising the driving age
    B   graduated driving licence
    C   the full licence scheme
    D   young British drivers' scheme

9   If the scheme is accepted what will be the minimum age at which anyone can drive alone?

A   25
B   21
C   18
D   17

10   There is a grammatical error on **Line 10**. Which words would correct this error?

A   has *welcomed*
B   whose *welcomed*
C   *have* welcomed
D   *proposal* is

11   Approximately how many people aged 17 to 25 are involved in accidents each year?

A   300
B   330
C   500
D   1000

12   When does the Government plan to set out its proposals for consideration?

A   Summer 2008
B   Spring 2008
C   Winter 2007
D   Winter 2008

Questions 13 to 20 relate to this letter

PETS SAFE AT HOME

Whiskers House, Pawsley, West Yorkshire WY23 9SC

01477 239887

petssafeathome@whiskers.co.uk

Mrs Moira Hartley
Seven Trees Cottage
Pear Tree Lane
BEXHILL ON SEA
Sussex   BX4 7AP

11 November 2007

Dear Madam

Thank you for your order for items from our Christmas Catalogue Sale, and your telephone call today.

We appologise that we sent you only one Collie Dog Calendar when your order clearly stated you wanted two of these. As we mentioned on the telephone, unfortunatly we are now out of stock of this item. Accordingly we are enclosing a check for £3.00 which is the cost of the calendar you did not receive.

As a gesture of goodwill, we hope you will accept a mug and coaster set with our compliments. These have been sent seperately and hopefully you will reciive them within the next three or four days.

Once more we are sorry for our error but hope you will continue to be a customer of **Pets Safe At Home**.

Yours faithfully

Sandra Sooty

Sandra Sooty
Customer Care Manager

Enc

13 The date is in the wrong place on the letter. Where should it be?

    A   at the end of the letter

    B   after "Dear Madam"

    C   before the name and address of the recipient

    D   before the Pets Safe At Home logo on the letterheading

14 The saluation is incorrect. How should this have been written?

    A   Dear Sir or Madam

    B   Dear Mrs Hartley

    C   Dear Mrs M Hartley

    D   Dear Hartley

15 There are three spelling mistakes in the second paragraph. Which words should be included in order to correct these errors?

    A   apologise, Calender, too

    B   Calender, telefone, unfortunately

    C   apologise, unfortunately, cheque

    D   Acorddingly, cheque, receive

16 There are two spelling mistakes in the third paragraph. Which words should be included in order to correct this error?

    A   jesture, complimments

    B   complimments, seperatly

    C   receive, separately

    D   seprately, for

17 The complimentary close is incorrect. How should this have been written?

    A   Yours Faithfully

    B   yours faithfully

    C   Yours sincerely

    D   Yours Sincerely

18 What is the purpose of the letter?

    A   to apologise for a mistake and offer a refund and a gift

    B   to apologise and send a refund

    C   to complain the customer ordered the wrong number of items

    D   to encourage the customer to buy more from the catalogue

19 What has been sent with the letter?

A a refund of £3.00
B a cup and saucer set
C a mug and coaster set
D a mug and coaster set and a £3.00 refund

20 What is the name of the person receiving the letter?

A Sandra Sooty
B Sandra Hartley
C Moira Hartley
D Moira Sooty

Questions 21 to 25 relate to this concert timetable

PACIFIC MOTORS : UK TOUR 2008

WELCOME TO THE PACIFIC MOTORS UK TOUR

DATE	CITY	VENUE
17 April	Birmingham	NEC Arena
18 April	Birmingham	NEC Arena
6 April	Belfast	NEC
24 April	Edinburgh	Arena
22 April	Glasgow	Arena
29 April	London	Millennium Dome
30 April	London	Millennium Dome
4 April	Manchester	Arena
26 April	Newcastle upon Tyne	Metro Radio Arena
19 April	Sheffield	Arena

21 A better way of arranging the tour dates is in datal order. When this is done, which **City** will appear second on the list?

A Sheffield
B Manchester
C Newcastle upon Tyne
D Belfast

22 How many cities host more than one concert?

    A   1

    B   2

    C   3

    D   none

23 What is the name of the group/band?

    A   Pacific Motors UK

    B   Motors

    C   Pacific Motors

    D   Pacific UK

24 After appearing in which **City** does the group/band have the longest rest before the next concert?

    A   Newcastle upon Tyne

    B   Edinburgh

    C   Sheffield

    D   Belfast

25 Which cities **start** and **end** the UK tour?

    A   Manchester and Belfast

    B   Belfast and Newcastle upon Tyne

    C   Sheffield and Edinburgh

    D   Manchester and London

Questions 26 to 35 are related to the text **Justwings.com**

JUSTWINGS.COM

MID-SEASON FLIGHT SALE

DON'T MISS THESE EXCEPTIONAL DEALS*
On sale from 09:00 am 11th May

Airport	Destination	Cost per person	Number of flights per week
BELFAST CITY AIRPORT**	Manchester	£21.99	20
	Exeter	£21.99	7
	Liverpool	£19.99	14
	Aberdeen	£22.00	10
BIRMINGHAM	Glasgow	£19.99	23
	Edinburgh	£19.99	25
	Jersey, CI	£31.99	10
	Guernsey, CI	£35.99	8
SOUTHAMPTON	Manchester	£21.99	18
	Liverpool	£21.00	10
	Dublin	£24.99	14
	Edinburgh	£21.99	30
BRISTOL	Belfast City	£29.99	7
	Jersey, CI	£31.00	7
MANCHESTER	Exeter	£21.99	12
	Belfast City	£21.99	20
NEWCASTLE	Belfast City	£19.99	7
	Exeter	£21.99	10
	Southampton	£21.99	14

All flight prices are one-way

* LAST DAY OF PURCHASE 1ST JUNE
** Renamed 22 May 2006 *George Best Belfast City Airport*

15% off Advantage Car hire when you book your air flight

26 It was intended that the **Airports** column was to be arranged in alphabetical order. Which airport is out of place in the list?

A Bristol
B Birmingham
C Southampton
D Manchester

27 Which is the most expensive flight?

A Southampton to Dublin
B Birmingham to Jersey
C Birmingham to Guernsey
D Newcastle to Belfast City

28 When does the mid-season flight sale end?

A 1st June
B 22nd May
C 30th May
D 11th May

29 Flights from Birmingham visit which city most often each week?

A Glasgow
B Edinburgh
C Jersey
D Guernsey

30 What is special about Belfast City Airport?

A it has the most flights each week
B is was renamed on 22nd May 2006
C is has the cheapest flights
D it used to be called George Best Belfast Airport

31 How many airports include flights to Jersey?

A 1
B 2
C 3
D 4

32 When do the flights begin to be sold?

A   9 pm on 1st June
B   9 am on 22nd May
C   9 pm on 11th May
D   9 am on 11th May

33 If someone wanted to buy a return ticket from Southampton to Liverpool, how much would it cost?

A   £21.00
B   £42.00
C   £210.00
D   £12.00

34 What is the advantage of booking a hire car when buying a ticket?

A   you can drive away from the airport
B   you can collect the car at the airport
C   there is a 5% discount
D   there is a 15% discount

35 What is the name of the company operating these flights?

A   Advantage
B   Mid-Season Flights
C   Just Wings
D   Wings

Questions 36 to 40 relate to **Helping the Hedgehog**

HELPING THE HEDGEHOG

The hedgehog is our only native spine-covered mammal but their numbers are decreasing because of the loss of their natural habitat. Many hedgehogs now rely on our gardens to forage, breed and hibernate.

A pile of leaves and twigs is an attractive home for a hedgehog, **but** what if it's a bonfire pile due to be part of the celebrations on Bonfire Night?

SOME SIMPLE RULES TO HELP SAVE A HIBERNATING HEDGEHOG

- Build the fire as close as possible to Bonfire night
- Make the pile of material next to where you intend to have the bonfire and rebuild the stack before lighting it
- Search under the fire using a torch and rake just before you light it
- If you find a hedgehog move it to somewhere dry and safe
- Consider making an alternative home by raking up grass cuttings or leaves into a pile a safe distance from the fire

FEEDING HEDGEHOGS

Remember don't give hedgehogs bread or milk as these are bad for them.

36 What is the **main** purpose of the document?

   A   to advise readers about how to keep hedgehogs safe, especially around bonfires

   B   to guide people on how to make hedgehogs feel at home in their garden

   C   to advise people how to feed hedgehogs

   D   to encourage people to make bonfires on 5 November

37 The word **decreasing** is used in the first paragraph. What alternative word could be used without altering the meaning of the text?

   A   growing

   B   falling

   C   jumping

   D   worrying

38   Why is it suggested that hedgehog numbers are decreasing?

    A   because they get burnt when bonfires are lit

    B   people are feeding them wrongly

    C   their natural habitat is being lost

    D   gardeners are not friendly towards them

39   If searching under a bonfire pile to see if a hedgehog is there before lighting it, what should you use?

    A   a torch

    B   a rake

    C   a torch and a rake

    D   a broom

40   The article says what you should not feed hedgehogs. To be really helpful to the reader what information should the article then go on to say?

    A   what you can give hedgehogs to eat

    B   what to do if you find a sick hedgehog

    C   how to care for a sick hedgehog

    D   what baby hedgehogs eat

END OF PAPER ELEVEN   END OF PAPER ELEVEN

END OF PAPER ELEVEN

Practice Multiple-choice Paper
suitable for:

Key Skills Level 1 Communication;
Level 1 Adult Literacy (Basic Skills); and
ESOL Skills for Life Level 1 Reading

Paper Twelve

YOU NEED
- This test paper.
- A pen.
- A pencil and eraser.
- An Answer Sheet.

You may NOT use a dictionary.
There are 40 questions on this paper. Try to answer ALL the questions.
When you have completed the questions you must check your answers,
then check them again.

YOU HAVE ONE HOUR TO FINISH THE PAPER

INSTRUCTIONS
- Make sure you write your name and today's date on the Answer
  Sheet. Use a pen to do this.
- Use a pencil to mark your answers so if you change your mind you
  can erase your choice and select another.
- Make sure that for each question you have only selected one
  answer. If you select more than one, the answer will not be
  marked.
- Read each question carefully before you select an answer.

Note for learners and tutors: This is a practice test that has been
designed to closely resemble the questions and question styles of a
"live" paper.

Questions 1 to 7 relate to this document

JUMBO DIY HYPERMARKET

AUTUMN SALE

20% OFF ENERGY-SAVING LIGHT BULBS (WHILST STOCKS LAST)

30% OFF SATIN FINISH EMULSION PAINT (ALL COLOURS)

35% OFF BRILLIANT WHITE GLOSS PAINT

30% OFF SELECTED WORKWEAR (including overalls, waterproof jackets* and safety helmets)

20% OFF "SUPERSPEED" POWER DRILLS
The Superspeed AK17 is supplied with
- **3 batteries**
- **A 1-year manufacturer's guarantee**

The AK17 is ideal for wood, metal and plastic and has two speed settings together with forward and reverse actions.

SALE BEGINS 25TH OCTOBER
M U S T   E N D   28TH OCTOBER AT 17:30

* AVAILABLE IN NAVY, BURGUNDY AND SLATE

1   How can the document best be described?

    A   a poster
    B   an advertisement
    C   a memorandum
    D   a notice

2   How many items are offered with **20% off**?

    A   1
    B   2
    C   3
    D   4

3   How much discount is there on white gloss paint?

    A   20%
    B   30%
    C   35%
    D   40%

4   Which item is available in three colours?

    A   the safety helmets
    B   the drill
    C   the pain
    D   the waterproof jackets

5   Which of the items is suitable for using with wood, plastic and metal?

    A   the paint
    B   the waterproof jackets
    C   the drill
    D   the safety helmets

6   When does the sale begin?

    A   28th October
    B   27th October
    C   24th October
    D   25th October

7 Where should anyone interested in purchasing any item go?

    A   Hypermarket
    B   DIY Hypermarket
    C   Jumbo Hypermarket
    D   Jumbo DIY Hypermarket

Questions 8 to 17 relate to this document

 # PETS SAFE AT HOME

To   Adrian Patchley

From   Sandra Sooty

Date   14 /02/2008

Re   **Pet-sitting requests for the month of March**

The following requests have come into the office in the last four days. I have confirmed the bookings with each client.

Client's name	Type of Pet	Inclusive Dates
Dr and Mrs P Yates	2 cats	5 – 11
Miss L Harrison	3 hamsters	3 – 14
Professor and Mrs P Fenton	2 dogs and a rabbit	15 – 28
Mr N Wilson	4 cats	23 – 29
Miss S Putman	5 cats and 2 dogs	11 – 19
Mrs I Iceton	1 parrot	4 – 17

Would you know please enter these details on the Booking Register and then match the bookings to our "Pet Sitters" and issue contract's to them.

Please let me have a copy of the Booking Register and the contracts when you have completed these tasks.

If you have any questions please contact me.

Thank you

Sandra

---

8   Of what type of document is this an example?

   A   a business letter
   B   a telephone message
   C   a memo
   D   a notice

9   The date has been incorrectly written. How should it appear?

   A   14 Feb 08
   B   14 Feb 2008
   C   14 Febrary 2007
   D   14 February 2008

10   For which month have the bookings been made?

   A   January
   B   March
   C   April
   D   May

11   What is the name of the member of staff who has to do the work?

   A   Sandra Sooty
   B   Sandra Patchley
   C   Adrian Patchley
   D   Andrew Patchley

12   If the names of the clients were arranged in alphabetical order, which client would come first on the list?

   A   Mrs I Iceton
   B   Miss S Putman
   C   Professor and Mrs P Fenton
   D   Miss L Harrison

13   If the booking **dates** were arranged in datal order, which date would come second?

   A   5 - 11
   B   3 - 14
   C   4 - 17
   D   11 - 19

14 In total, how many cats require pet sitting?

    A   6

    B   7

    C   9

    D   11

15 What is the **first** job to be done by the person who receives the document?

    A   complete the Booking Register

    B   issue contracts to the pet sitters

    C   telephone the sender to ask for instructions

    D   contact the clients and confirm the bookings

16 What documents does Sandra Sooty want to receive?

    A   the contracts

    B   the Booking Register

    C   the Booking Register and the contracts

    D   the confirmation of the bookings sent to the clients

17 There is a spelling and a punctuation error in the paragraph that begins **Would you**. Which words should be included to correct these errors?

    A   Redgister, booking's

    B   now, contracts'

    C   two, Sitters'

    D   now, contracts

Questions 18 to 24 relate to this document

THE WAITING ROOM RESTAURANT*

PROGRAMME OF SPRING EVENTS

THE WAITING ROOM in Eggleton is a very popular and homely restaurant that serves award-winning food as well as hosting live music evenings each Saturday. We call these music evenings "Saturday night – Sunday morning".

Spring Programme

1 March – 13 March A lively band of 5 singing hits from the movies	**Badgers' Sett**
23 March – 27 March The best of local folk	**The John John Band**
7 April – 15 April Four play classical pop	**Colm Martin Quartet**
3 May – 11 May Songs from the 70s and 80s	**Hope Springs Eternal**

SAMPLE VEGETARIAN MENU
£10.00 per person

Warm Moroccan Dip, with Pita Bread,
Pear and Stilton Salad

Spinach, Feta and Mushroom Curry with Potato Kibbeh
Red Thai Bean Curry**

Ginger Crumble
Lemon Meringue Pie

* The National Courier Food Award Winner 2006
** £3.50 extra

**The Waiting Room, 81 Station Road, Eggleton
01852 586239**

18   Which Award did the restaurant win in 2006?

    A   The Courier Award for Food
    B   The Courier Restaurant Award
    C   The National Award for Food
    D   The National Courier Food Award

19   What is the name given to the music evenings?

    A   Waiting for Saturday night
    B   Waiting around for Sunday morning
    C   Saturday night – Sunday morning
    D   The Waiting Room entertainment

20   On what night is the music entertainment?

    A   Saturday
    B   Sunday
    C   every night
    D   Friday

21   Which band/group specialises in folk music?

    A   Hope Springs Eternal
    B   Colm Martin Quartet
    C   Badgers' Sett
    D   The John John Band

22   If you booked for 24 March, which group/band would you hear?

    A   Colm Martin Quartet
    B   The John John Band
    C   Hope Springs Eternal
    D   Badgers' Sett

23   If you wanted a main course of Red Thai Bean Curry, how much would your full meal cost?

    A   £12.50
    B   £13.00
    C   £13.50
    D   £3.50

24 What do you think is the reason for the picture of the train on the document?

A   the owners like trains

B   it serves express food

C   the food is as good as you can get on a train

D   the restaurant is near a train station and stations have waiting rooms

Questions 25 to 31 relate to this text

THE IMPORTANCE OF VINEGAR

SOME OF THE USES OF VINEGAR

In the house

- Get rid of germs
- Disinfect and deodorise
- Clean carpets and rugs
- Clean windows and mirrors
- Remove ink, coffee, rust, red and white wine stains
- Polish chrome, brass, copper and leather

In the laundry

- Return colours to their original intensity
- Give all your white linen a sparkle
- Remove perspiration and deodorant stains
- Prevent clothes becoming shiny when ironing

In the kitchen

- Destroy bacteria
- Give glasses and china a lovely sparkle
- Refresh old saucepans
- Disinfect the refrigerator, chopping boards and kitchen utensils
- Clean the oven without having to scrub it

In gardens, yards and garages

- Repel insects
- Protect plants from ants
- Prevent and combat mildew
- Get rid of weeds

For a healthy body

- A refreshing bath tonic
- Remove dandruff
- Treat wasp stings

- -

For further information on the uses and value of vinegar, send for a free booklet

To Spring and Cutler Ltd, Dept 26, Brunel Road, Bristol, Avon BT3 5JM

Name .... Address ....

.... Post Code ....

Visit www.scltdproducts.com

25   What is the purpose of the text?

   ✗ **A**   to inform
     B   to persuade readers to buy vinegar
   ☐ **C**   to inform and offer a free booklet
     D   to sell the booklet on vinegar

26   The word **deodorise** is used in the second bullet point in the "In the house" paragraph. Which alternative word could be used without altering the meaning of the text?

   A   freshen
   B   smell
   C   freshening
   D   cleaning

27   What use can vinegar be when ironing?

   A   it will stop the iron overheating
   B   it prevents mildew on the iron
   C   it makes creases more sharp
   D   it prevents clothes becoming shiny

28   What will vinegar do to glassware?

   A   make it shine
   B   prevent it from being scratched
   C   prevent mildew
   D   remove wine stains

29   Apart from using vinegar to polish brass, what other items can be polished with it?

   A   leather and copper
   B   chrome and copper
   C   tin, copper and leather
   D   leather, copper and chrome

30   If a reader wanted more information what are they asked to do?

   A   telephone for a booklet
   B   pay £9.99 for a booklet
   C   send for a free booklet and consult the company's website
   D   look up information in a book

31 What is the name for the part of the form placed at **A**?

  A an invitation
  B a tear-off slip
  C an advertisement
  D a brochure

Questions 32 to 36 relate to this text

AIRE VALLEY
WOODLAND WALK

No. 2 in the series of 11

5½ mile Circular Walk (8.8km)

A level walk through beautiful countryside taking in the Leeds and Liverpool Canal, the River Aire, Bingley, Hirst Woods and the Victorian streets of Saltaire.

The Route

At the southern end of Victoria Road turn left onto the canal towpath. Follow the towpath for ½ mile to Hirst Lock. Cross the stile to the west of the Lock and follow the path straight ahead and over the metal footbridge spanning the River Aire. Turn left and continue straight ahead along the riverbank. The river will be on your right and the Bradford Rowing Club building on your left.

Walk for approximately 3 miles until you cross the canal at Bridge No. 708. Turn right when you leave the bridge and walk under Bridge No. 707. This bridge spans both the canal and the Bingley Main Road. Turn left to leave the canal towpath at Marker 18. Cross Bingley High Street via the Pelican Crossing and turn right outside Carters' Cosmetics and walk up Ferncliffe Road to the traffic lights at the junction of Bingley High Street and East Wynd.

Hints

Comfortable, strong walking shoes are recommended along with outdoor clothing to suit the season.

A light snack is advisable.

Please take care when leaving the towpath and entering Bingley High Street.

---

32 Which canal is mentioned in the text?

  A Aire and Bingley
  B Leeds and Bingley
  C Leeds and Liverpool
  D Liverpool and Leeds

33 How can the text best be described?

    A   a leaflet to give information and to guide people
    B   an instruction for walkers
    C   a publicity leaflet
    D   an advertising leaflet for Bingley

34 Where is the stile situated?

    A   west of the lock
    B   ahead of the metal footbridge
    C   at the end of Victoria Road
    D   beside Marker 18

35 The word "spanning" is used in the second paragraph. ".... the metal footbridge spanning the River Aire." Which alternative word or phrase could be used without altering the meaning of the text?

    A   extent
    B   extending
    C   reaching
    D   extending over

36 What is the walker going to do when they approach Marker 18?

    A   leave the towpath
    B   cross a road
    C   walk across a bridge
    D   walk underneath a bridge

Question 37 relates to the table and the charts A, B, C and D

Porto Santo Lines have kept a record of ferry cruise bookings in June and July. These are shown in the table

MONTH	NO. OF PASSENGERS WITH VEHICLES	NO. OF FOOT PASSENGERS
June	3,500	5,600
July	4,690	8,300

37 Which of the charts accurately reflects the information shown in the table for the months indicated?

A   A
B   B
C   C
D   D

Chart A

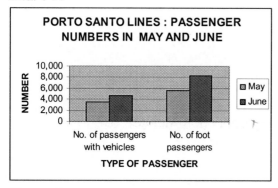

Chart B

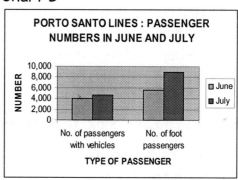

Chart C

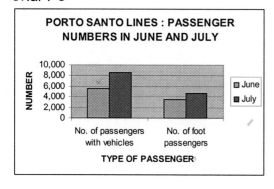

Chart D

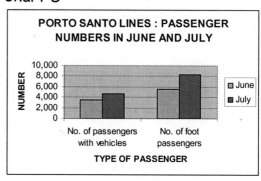

Questions 38 to 40 relate to spelling and punctuation

38   Which of the following sentences uses correct spelling and apostrophes?

   A   If wer'e going to the fair on Saterday, then let's hope its good weather.

   B   If we're going to the fair on Saterday, then lets hope its' good whether.

   C   If we're going to the fair on Saturday, then let's hope it's good weather.

   D   If were going to the fair on Saturday, then lets hope it's good whether.

39   Which of the following sentences uses correct spelling?

   A   Febrary is usually a cold month but in Australia it is there autum and warmer than hear.

   B   Febary is usually a cold month but in Australia it is there autumn and warmer than here.

   C   Febury is usually a cold month but in Australia it is their autummn and warmer than hear.

   D   February is usually a cold month but in Australia it is their autumn and warmer than here.

40   Which of the following sentences uses correct spelling and apostrophes?

   A   Bargain Price Department Store has lady's handbags' in there sale. There're a good perchase.

   B   Bargain Price Departtment Store has ladies handbag's in their sale. They're a good purchase.

   C   Bargain Price Department Store has ladies' handbags in their sale. They're a good purchase.

   D   Bargain Price Department Store has ladys' handbags in their sale. There're a good perchase.

END OF PAPER TWELVE   END OF PAPER TWELVE

END OF PAPER TWELVE

Answers

MULTIPLE-CHOICE QUESTIONS : LEVEL 1

Question	Answer	Question	Answer	Question	Answer
		PAPER ONE			
1	B	2	C	3	B
4	B	5	C	6	A
7	B	8	B	9	B
10	C	11	C	12	A
13	D	14	B	15	D
16	A	17	B	18	C
19	D	20	B	21	C
22	A	23	C	24	D
25	A	26	B	27	C
28	D	29	D	30	C
31	D	32	B	33	C
34	D	35	C	36	B
37	A	38	C	39	D
40	B				
		PAPER TWO			
1	B	2	D	3	B
4	D	5	C	6	D
7	D	8	B	9	C
10	D	11	D	12	B
13	C	14	B	15	B
16	D	17	A	18	A
19	C	20	B	21	C
22	C	23	A	24	C
25	C	26	D	27	C
28	C	29	C	30	B
31	C	32	D	33	D
34	C	35	A	36	B
37	D	38	A	39	B
40	C				
		PAPER THREE			
1	D	2	D	3	C
4	C	5	D	6	B
7	D	8	B	9	B
10	A	11	B	12	C
13	D	14	C	15	C
16	B	17	C	18	B
19	D	20	D	21	B
22	D	23	C	24	C
25	D	26	C	27	D
28	D	29	B	30	B
31	B	32	C	33	C
34	B	35	C	36	D
37	C	38	A	39	B
40	D				
		PAPER FOUR			
1	C	2	B	3	A
4	D	5	B	6	C
7	C	8	B	9	C
10	A	11	A	12	C
13	D	14	C	15	D
16	C	17	D	18	B
19	A	20	D	21	C
22	D	23	D	24	B
25	D	26	B	27	B
28	C	29	A	30	B
31	C	32	B	33	B
34	C	35	B	36	C
37	C	38	B	39	C
40	A				

MULTIPLE-CHOICE QUESTIONS : LEVEL 1

Question	Answer	Question	Answer	Question	Answer
		PAPER FIVE			
1	A	2	C	3	C
4	B	5	B	6	B
7	C	8	A	9	A
10	B	11	C	12	D
13	B	14	A	15	B
16	D	17	B	18	B
19	C	20	D	21	C
22	A	23	C	24	D
25	B	26	D	27	B
28	D	29	C	30	D
31	C	32	A	33	B
34	C	35	A	36	D
37	B	38	B	39	D
40	C				
		PAPER SIX			
1	C	2	C	3	C
4	B	5	C	6	B
7	C	8	D	9	B
10	D	11	D	12	C
13	B	14	B	15	C
16	C	17	D	18	C
19	A	20	B	21	C
22	B	23	D	24	C
25	A	26	B	27	D
28	B	29	C	30	B
31	C	32	D	33	C
34	D	35	B	36	C
37	D	38	D	39	C
40	A				
		PAPER SEVEN			
1	B	2	C	3	C
4	A	5	C	6	C
7	C	8	B	9	B
10	C	11	B	12	D
13	D	14	C	15	D
16	B	17	A	18	D
19	A	20	C	21	B
22	A	23	C	24	D
25	C	26	D	27	A
28	D	29	B	30	C
31	B	32	C	33	C
34	C	35	D	36	B
37	C	38	D	39	C
40	A				
		PAPER EIGHT			
1	B	2	B	3	C
4	C	5	D	6	C
7	A	8	B	9	D
10	C	11	A	12	B
13	A	14	C	15	C
16	C	17	D	18	C
19	D	20	D	21	A
22	C	23	C	24	D
25	B	26	D	27	B
28	C	29	C	30	D
31	D	32	B	33	B
34	C	35	A	36	B
37	C	38	B	39	D
40	B				

MULTIPLE-CHOICE QUESTIONS : LEVEL 1

Question	Answer	Question	Answer	Question	Answer
		PAPER NINE			
1	C	2	D	3	B
4	D	5	B	6	C
7	D	8	A	9	A
10	C	11	C	12	B
13	D	14	B	15	B
16	D	17	B	18	C
19	B	20	C	21	D
22	C	23	A	24	C
25	C	26	D	27	D
28	C	29	B	30	C
31	B	32	D	33	C
34	D	35	D	36	C
37	B	38	D	39	A
40	C				
		PAPER TEN			
1	D	2	B	3	D
4	A	5	C	6	C
7	C	8	B	9	B
10	C	11	B	12	D
13	C	14	A	15	C
16	D	17	C	18	C
19	B	20	B	21	C
22	C	23	D	24	C
25	A	26	D	27	C
28	D	29	A	30	C
31	A	32	D	33	B
34	D	35	B	36	C
37	B	38	D	39	B
40	A				
		PAPER ELEVEN			
1	D	2	B	3	C
4	A	5	D	6	D
7	D	8	B	9	C
10	C	11	D	12	C
13	C	14	B	15	C
16	C	17	C	18	A
19	A	20	C	21	D
22	B	23	C	24	D
25	D	26	C	27	C
28	A	29	B	30	B
31	B	32	D	33	B
34	D	35	C	36	A
37	B	38	C	39	C
40	A				
		PAPER TWELVE			
1	B	2	B	3	C
4	D	5	C	6	D
7	D	8	C	9	D
10	B	11	C	12	C
13	C	14	D	15	A
16	C	17	D	18	D
19	C	20	A	21	D
22	B	23	C	24	D
25	C	26	A	27	D
28	A	29	D	30	C
31	B	32	C	33	A
34	A	35	D	36	A
37	D	38	C	39	D
40	C				

QUESTIONS DISTRIBUTION KEY

G	Grammar
L	Layout of document
M	Identify Main points and ideas
R	Rearranging text
S&P	Spelling and Punctuation
W	Style of Writing/Purpose of document
I	Interpreting graphs/charts/tables

PAPER ONE

Question	Key	Question	Key	Question	Key	Question	Key
1	G	2	M	3	M	4	M
5	M	6	G	7	M	8	L
9	L	10	S&P	11	S&P	12	M
13	M	14	L	15	M/L	16	I
17	I	18	M	19	M	20	M
21	M	22	M	23	M	24	G
25	G	26	G	27	M	28	W
29	S&P	30	S&P	31	S&P	32	M
33	R	34	M	35	M	36	M
37	G	38	M	39	G	40	M

PAPER TWO

Question	Key	Question	Key	Question	Key	Question	Key
1	M	2	M	3	M	4	M
5	M	6	M	7	M	8	M
9	M	10	W	11	M	12	S&P
13	G	14	M	15	S&P	16	M
17	M	18	R/I	19	I	20	I
21	I	22	I	23	M/W	24	G
25	M	26	M	27	S&P	28	M
29	W	30	M	31	I	32	I
33	S&P	34	S&P	35	S&P	36	M
37	M	38	G	39	G	40	M

PAPER THREE

Question	Key	Question	Key	Question	Key	Question	Key
1	S&P	2	I	3	M	4	I
5	S&P	6	I	7	W	8	R
9	I	10	M	11	I	12	I
13	I	14	I	15	R	16	R
17	R	18	I	19	I	20	W
21	M	22	S&P	23	M	24	M
25	S&P	26	S&P	27	S&P/G	28	W
29	M	30	M	31	M	32	M
33	M	34	M	35	M	36	M
37	M	38	M	39	M	40	I

PAPER FOUR

Question	Key	Question	Key	Question	Key	Question	Key
1	W	2	G	3	M	4	S&P
5	M	6	M	7	M	8	M
9	M	10	M	11	G	12	M
13	S&P	14	S&P	15	M	16	I
17	I	18	I	19	I	20	I
21	M	22	M	23	M	24	G
25	M	26	M	27	S&P	28	M
29	W	30	M	31	M	32	M
33	M	34	M	35	L	36	L
37	M	38	S&P	39	S&P	40	W

QUESTIONS DISTRIBUTION KEY

G	Grammar
L	Layout of document
M	Identify Main points and ideas
R	Rearranging text
S&P	Spelling and Punctuation
W	Style of Writing/Purpose of document
I	Interpreting graphs/charts/tables

PAPER FIVE

Question	Key	Question	Key	Question	Key	Question	Key
1	I/R	2	I	3	I	4	I
5	M	6	I	7	I	8	I
9	W	10	M	11	M	12	M
13	M	14	M	15	S&P	16	W
17	I	18	I	19	I	20	I
21	I/M	22	M	23	I	24	I
25	M	26	I	27	M	28	M
29	M	30	M	31	M	32	S&P
33	M	34	M	35	S&P	36	M
37	G	38	M	39	W	40	M

PAPER SIX

Question	Key	Question	Key	Question	Key	Question	Key
1	S&P	2	S&P	3	S&P	4	M
5	M	6	M	7	G	8	G
9	M	10	W	11	I	12	I
13	I	14	I	15	I	16	L
17	S&P	18	L	19	G	20	M
21	S&P	22	L	23	I/M	24	W
25	G	26	M	27	M	28	M
29	I/M	30	W	31	L	32	M
33	M	34	M	35	M	36	M
37	G	38	S&P	39	S&P	40	W

PAPER SEVEN

Question	Key	Question	Key	Question	Key	Question	Key
1	S&P	2	G	3	S&P	4	S&P
5	W	6	M	7	G	8	W
9	M	10	M	11	G	12	M
13	M	14	W	15	M	16	M
17	M	18	M	19	I	20	I
21	I	22	I	23	I/R	24	I
25	I	26	L	27	S&P	28	W
29	G	30	L	31	M	32	W
33	W	34	M	35	S&P	36	M
37	M	38	M	39	M	40	M

PAPER EIGHT

Question	Key	Question	Key	Question	Key	Question	Key
1	W	2	G	3	M	4	G
5	S&P	6	M	7	G/M	8	M
9	S&P	10	S&P	11	S&P	12	S&P
13	G	14	S&P	15	M	16	M
17	M	18	M	19	G	20	M
21	S&P	22	I	23	I	24	I
25	I	26	I	27	M	28	M
29	S&P	30	M	31	I	32	W
33	M	34	M	35	G	36	M
37	M	38	M	39	M	40	W

QUESTIONS DISTRIBUTION KEY

G	Grammar
L	Layout of document
M	Identify Main points and ideas
R	Rearranging text
S&P	Spelling and Punctuation
W	Style of Writing/Purpose of document
I	Interpreting graphs/charts/tables

PAPER NINE

Question	Key	Question	Key	Question	Key	Question	Key
1	W	2	M	3	S&P	4	S&P
5	S&P	6	M	7	L	8	L/M
9	S&P	10	W	11	M	12	M
13	M	14	M	15	M	16	L
17	M	18	W	19	M	20	I
21	I	22	M	23	G	24	W
25	W	26	L	27	R	28	R
29	M	30	M	31	I	32	S&P/G
33	S&P/G	34	S&P/G	35	M	36	S&P
37	G	38	M	39	S&P	40	M

PAPER TEN

Question	Key	Question	Key	Question	Key	Question	Key
1	M	2	M	3	M	4	M
5	M	6	M	7	I	8	W
9	S&P	10	S&P	11	S&P	12	M
13	I/R	14	I	15	I	16	I
17	R	18	L	19	M	20	S&P
21	M	22	M	23	M	24	L
25	M/L	26	M	27	S&P	28	M
29	W	30	M	31	W	32	M
33	M	34	M	35	M	36	M
37	G	38	M	39	M	40	M

PAPER ELEVEN

Question	Key	Question	Key	Question	Key	Question	Key
1	S&P	2	W	3	M	4	G
5	G	6	M	7	S&P	8	M
9	M	10	G	11	M	12	M
13	L	14	L	15	S&P	16	S&P
17	L	18	W	19	M	20	L/M
21	R	22	I	23	M	24	I
25	I	26	R	27	I	28	M
29	I	30	M	31	I	32	M
33	M	34	M	35	M	36	W
37	G	38	M	39	M	40	M

PAPER TWELVE

Question	Key	Question	Key	Question	Key	Question	Key
1	W	2	M	3	M	4	M
5	M	6	M	7	M	8	W
9	L	10	M	11	M	12	I/R
13	I/R	14	I	15	M	16	M
17	S&P	18	M	19	M	20	M
21	M	22	M	23	M	24	M
25	W	26	G	27	M	28	M
29	M	30	M	31	L	32	M
33	W	34	M	35	G	36	M
37	I	38	S&P	39	S&P	40	S&P

ANSWER GRID

Name ....   Date ....

Instructions

Select **one** answer choice for each question.

Mark your chosen letter answer with a horizontal line **in pencil**.

If you wish to change an answer to a question, erase your first choice and select another letter.

1 [a] [b] [c] [d]	2 [a] [b] [c] [d]	3 [a] [b] [c] [d]	4 [a] [b] [c] [d]	5 [a] [b] [c] [d]
6 [a] [b] [c] [d]	7 [a] [b] [c] [d]	8 [a] [b] [c] [d]	9 [a] [b] [c] [d]	10 [a] [b] [c] [d]
11 [a] [b] [c] [d]	12 [a] [b] [c] [d]	13 [a] [b] [c] [d]	14 [a] [b] [c] [d]	15 [a] [b] [c] [d]
16 [a] [b] [c] [d]	17 [a] [b] [c] [d]	18 [a] [b] [c] [d]	19 [a] [b] [c] [d]	20 [a] [b] [c] [d]
21 [a] [b] [c] [d]	22 [a] [b] [c] [d]	23 [a] [b] [c] [d]	24 [a] [b] [c] [d]	25 [a] [b] [c] [d]
26 [a] [b] [c] [d]	27 [a] [b] [c] [d]	28 [a] [b] [c] [d]	29 [a] [b] [c] [d]	30 [a] [b] [c] [d]
31 [a] [b] [c] [d]	32 [a] [b] [c] [d]	33 [a] [b] [c] [d]	34 [a] [b] [c] [d]	35 [a] [b] [c] [d]
36 [a] [b] [c] [d]	37 [a] [b] [c] [d]	38 [a] [b] [c] [d]	39 [a] [b] [c] [d]	40 [a] [b] [c] [d]

Lightning Source UK Ltd.
Milton Keynes UK
UKOW010155220312

189397UK00001B/12/A